P9-CBX-881

Dr Gareth Moore is the author of over 25 brain-training and puzzle books for both children and adults, including *The Mammoth Book of Brain Workouts*. His brain training material has also appeared in a wide range of newspapers and magazines.

He writes and runs the monthly logic puzzle magazine *Sudoku Xtra*, as well as the popular online puzzle site *PuzzleMix.com*.

He gained his Ph.D at the University of Cambridge, UK, where he taught machines to recognise the English language.

More brain training material can be found at his website, *DrGarethMoore.com*.

Also available

Fun THE MAMMOTH BOOK OF BRAIN TRAINING

Dr Gareth Moore

ROBINSON

RUNNING PRESS
PHILADELPHIA · LONDON

Constable & Robinson Ltd
3 The Lanchesters
162 Fulham Palace Road
London W6 9ER
www.constablerobinson.com

First published in the UK by Robinson,
an imprint of Constable & Robinson, 2011

Copyright © Dr Gareth Moore, 2010

The right of Dr Gareth Moore to be identified as the
author of this work has been asserted by him in accordance
with the Copyright, Designs & Patents Act 1988.

All rights reserved. This book is sold subject to the condition
that it shall not, by way of trade or otherwise, be lent, re-sold,
hired out or otherwise circulated in any form of binding or cover
other than that in which it is published and without a similar condition
including this condition being imposed on the subsequent purchaser.

A copy of the British Library Cataloguing in Publication
Data is available from the British Library

UK ISBN 978-1-84901-434-2

1 3 5 7 9 10 8 6 4 2

First published in the United States in 2011 by Running Press Book Publishers

All rights reserved under the Pan-American and International Copyright
Conventions

This book may not be reproduced in whole or in part, in any form or by any
means, electronic or mechanical, including photocopying, recording, or by any
information storage and retrieval system now known or hereafter invented,
without written permission from the publisher.

9 8 7 6 5 4 3 2 1
Digit on the right indicates the number of this printing

US Library of Congress number: 2010925952
US ISBN 978-0-7624-4093-1

Running Press Book Publishers
2300 Chestnut Street
Philadelphia, PA 19103-4371

Visit us on the web!
www.runningpress.com

Printed and bound in China

>> Contents

This book is packed with an enormously wide cross-section of puzzles and fun brain challenges, guaranteed to keep you on your mental toes! And just try imagining what that would look like!

> 24 Weeks of Whole-Brain Goodness

Just like whole-grain bread is better for you than plain old white, so whole-brain training is heads (and tails) above the rest. In this book you'll find an equal amount of time is spent on each of the key mental skill areas:

Visualisation   Reasoning   Memory

Numbers   Words   Creativity

Each week you'll find one or two tasks in each of the above areas, so try to cover them all in an actual calendar week if you can, and don't be tempted to skip those you find tricky - these are most likely to be the ones that will lead to the best mental improvement! Spend just a few minutes every day or so on the workouts in this book and you'll be helping to keep your brain fully fed.

> Light Up Your Brain

If you'd like to keep track of your progress then you can use the amazing Light Up Your Brain[not-a-TM] system developed especially for this book. At the top of each workout are a number of light bulbs, representing the maximum number of points you can gain for that task. Once you've tried the task, simply check your solution against the one given at the back of the book, or for some of the memory workouts against the given items, and then deduct one point for each mistake you made. But you're doing the scoring, so use your common sense as to how many points to give yourself - use a minimum of one point per page.

600
500
400
300
200
100
50
25

At the top-right of each double-page brain workout you'll find a box to write the score you got for those pages and also a place to keep a running total of your score so far. At the end of each week turn to the very back page of the book and shade in the relevant ring of the Light Up Your Brain[still-not-a-TM] chart with a proportional number of points - so if you've got 75 points so far then you should shade in all of the 25 and 50 rings, and half of the 100 ring (since that ring takes 50 further points to fill). If you use orange and yellow felt-tips then you'll get that real Light Up Your Brain[shiny] illumination thrill.

If you somehow manage to score more than the 600 points the chart allows (there are 774 bulbs in the book) then you can start shading in the central chart bulb itself for any extra score.

> The Workouts

It's best to follow the book through in page order from the start to the end. I've made a real effort to mix up the content as much as possible throughout the weeks for a better brain training experience, and a few of the types that appear more than once contain more detailed instructions earlier on in the book than they do when featured later on. Note also that the difficulty level increases slowly throughout the book, so you should find it easier if you start at the beginning too.

31	27	23	19	21
29	25	21	17	11
33	39	43	13	15
37	41	19	15	19
49	45	21	25	29

46 〉 1/2 of this 〉 -17 〉 +4 〉 ×10 〉 RESULT

24 〉 -50% 〉 +9 〉 ÷3 〉 ×5 〉 RESULT

> Word Lists

For those word challenges where I provide a list of possible words at the back, these are for reference and not intended to be a complete list of every word you should aim to find. In general if I couldn't find a word in the Concise Oxford English Dictionary then I didn't list it, although there are some exceptions. Some of the words given are occasionally technical so you're very unlikely to know them all, and conversely you may well find words that aren't in my lists.

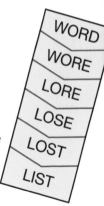

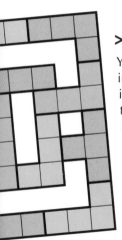

> Training Your Brain

Your brain is the most phenomenal learning machine in the known universe and it thrives on novelty, new ideas, new thoughts and new experiences. It's central to every idea we have and movement we make, so looking after it is key - and that's where brain training can come in.

Caring for your brain involves keeping yourself mentally stimulated. If your job or chosen path rarely challenges you, or you spend most of your time in the same physical locations, then it's about getting out there and seeing new things and doing new activities. Of course the realities of life make this somewhat impractical most of the time, and so this book is your next best bet!

> The Science Bit

Brain training theory states that you can practise one activity and through this gain general experience that allows you to become good at other activities too. There's plenty of debate about how powerful this effect is, with a key question being at what point do I stop gaining general experience and am simply getting better at the specific task I'm doing? So instead of repeated exercises, which may or may not help your brain, this book is instead full of an extremely wide and varied set of challenges.

It's a well-known fact that our brains learn best when we are genuinely interested in an activity, which is why everything in this book is intended to be fun. There are no pages of sums here, or mechanical tasks to perform. If you do find yourself getting stuck or frustrated on a workout then why not take a quick look at the solutions for a hint, or put the book down and come back to it later - it's amazing how much just taking a break can help! Your brain carries on thinking without your conscious effort - it really is amazing!

Original concept and all text, illustrations, design and layout by

Dr Gareth Moore
(online: www.DrGarethMoore.com)

For my Gran,
who showed me how to colour.

> Six-sided Imagination 🔦🔦🔦

Imagine that you cut each of these four shape nets out and then fold each one of them up to make a cube. Three of these shape nets make the same, identical cube, but the fourth is different. By visualising the position and orientation of each shape when folded, can you say which one is the odd one out?

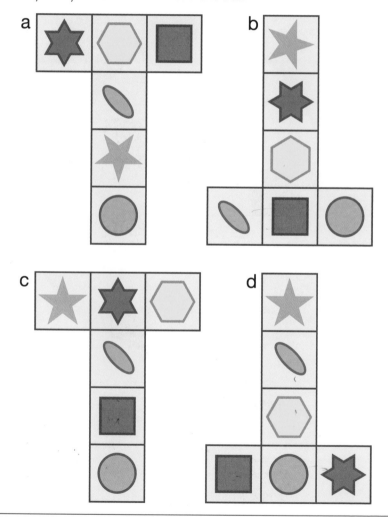

> Combined Approach

Mentally imagine combining the two images below, so the white squares on one are replaced with the contents of the coloured squares from the other.

> How many blue squares are there in the resulting image?

> How many red, yellow and green squares in total can you count in the combined image?

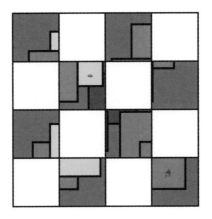

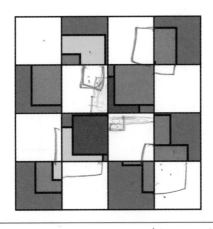

> Fences

Can you join all of the dots together into a single loop such that every dot is used? Only horizontal and vertical lines are allowed, and the loop cannot cross over or touch itself in any way.

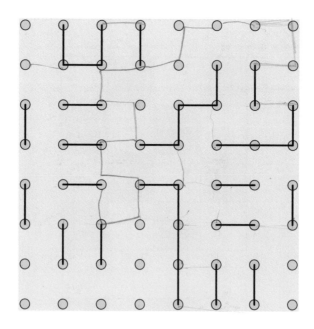

> Going around the loop again

If you find this puzzle straightforward then you're all set to try out the loop-making Slitherlink puzzles later on in this book! Although possibly the most pure logic puzzles ever devised, they can pose quite a challenge!

> Rectangles

Draw solid lines along the dashed lines in order to divide the grid up into a set of rectangles.
> The number inside each rectangle must be equal to the number of dashed-line squares it contains.
> Each rectangle must have exactly one number inside it.

> Box Clever

You can find more of these puzzles in some newspapers, where they are sometimes published as daily brain workouts. Some Japanese puzzle makers also create enormous 40x30 square versions - or larger!

> Remember the Difference

How good is your visual memory? Do you realise straight away when something has visibly changed, or do you need prompting?

In this memory task first of all cover the opposite page before studying the night-time scene below for no more than 30 seconds. Then cover over this page instead and reveal the opposite page, which you will need to rotate around to read, and follow the instructions there.

> Testing your Visual Memory

Look at the version of the picture on this page. Right away, how many differences can you see? Make a note of each difference and then only continue reading below when you can't find any more.

Here is a clue to each of the differences, if you could not already find them:
> Something at sea has changed colour
> Wasn't it night-time before?
> Isn't there sand by the sea sometimes?
> How quickly do plants grow?
> Water is very reflective.

Can you spot them all? If not, flip back to the original picture and see if you can spot all five now.

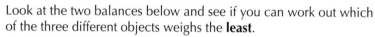

> Balancing Act

Look at the two balances below and see if you can work out which of the three different objects weighs the **least**.

Assume that distance from the fulcrum (the centre of the balance) has no effect on the result.

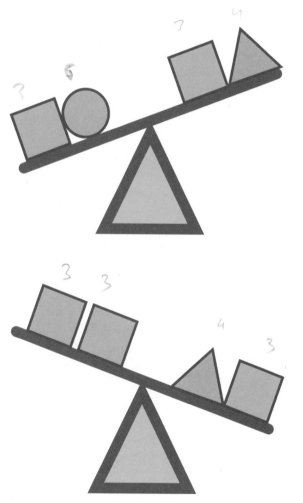

> Dealer's Luck?

A standard pack of 52 playing cards contains 13 each of 4 different suits, with A, 2, 3, 4, 5, 6, 7, 8, 9, 10, J, Q, K in each suit.

If you were to shuffle a pack and deal yourself a single card, the likelihood that the suit would be **spades** is 1 in 4. The likelihood that the card would be a **4** is 1 in 13. And the likelihood that you would get the **4 of spades** is 1 in 52.

Imagine you shuffle an ordinary 52-card pack and deal these three cards:

You next deal yourself a fourth card. What is the likelihood of each of the following alternatives?

> **A club**
> **A red card**
> **The 10 of spades**

If your fourth card had been the 5 of clubs, what is the likelihood that a fifth card would be a heart?

> Baby Blocks

Can you rearrange the floating sea of letters below into five baby animals? Each letter should be used exactly once in the resulting set.

> ## Spot the Pots? Stop for Post?

Each of these sentences contains some missing underlined words, each of which is an anagram of one another within that sentence.

Pick one set of letters from the following list for each sentence, and place a different anagram (that uses all of the letters in each case) into each gap. Each set is used only once.

A C D E R S

A D E L S T

I K N S

E I M S T

> At _____, one of the _____ _____ a strange noise.

> She is too _____ to visit the grove of _____ _____.

> Travelling through river _____, he hoped his water supply _Lasted_ as long as _____, and regretted eating so much _salted_ food.

> He washed his _sink_ in the _____ to remove the _____.

> And the Sky, Full of Stars

The night sky below is full of stars. Draw straight lines between them to design a constellation of your own.

One way to do this is to start with random lines, then take a step back to see what the result looks like so far and then continue from there.

Name your constellation:

> Star-gazing

Some people think they "aren't creative". If that's you then be sure to try the above exercise - you might discover you're more imaginative than you thought!

> Single Stroke

Can you draw this pattern in a single stroke without taking your pen off the paper or drawing any line more than once? Crossing an existing line is allowed.

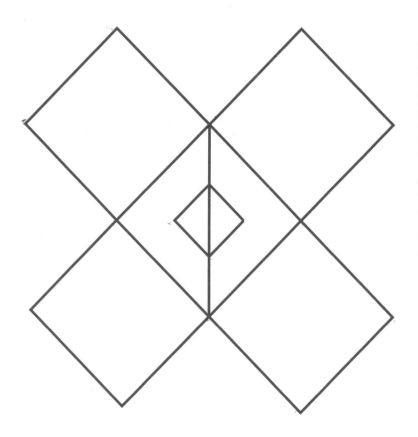

> **Burning Question**

If you set up six matches as shown here then you make one triangle and one square.

Can you move just three matches so that you end up with eight triangles instead? You may not break any of the matches into multiple pieces!

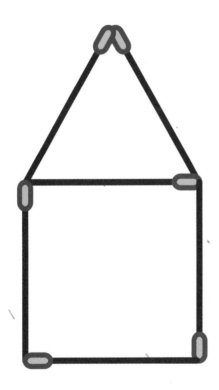

> Four by Four

Can you place 1 to 4 into each row and column of the grid to the right?

2	4	1	3
3	1	2	4
4	2	3	1
1	3	4	2

Now try the same with the grid below, while also obeying the inequality signs. The arrow must always point to the smaller number in each pair.

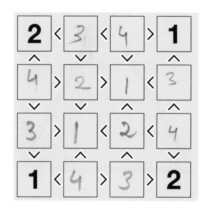

Try the same again with this grid, which has no 'given' numbers:

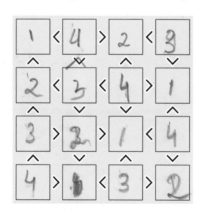

Can you do the same when you have far fewer inequality arrows?

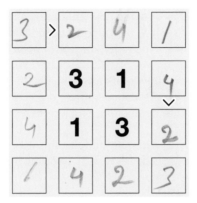

Finally, try this last puzzle with just a few inequalities and no given numbers at all!

> Futoshiki

This type of puzzle, with rows and columns to fill plus inequalities to obey, is usually known by its Japanese name of **Futoshiki**, meaning "inequality". You can find it in some newspapers.

>> MEMORY

> Joined-up Memory

Remembering lists of numbers may not be the most exciting task in the world but it's very useful to be able to recall certain bits of information rapidly, such as the price you expected to pay for an item, the house number you're looking for or even a phone number.

In this particular workout you'll know how you're doing because as you recall the numbers correctly you'll be drawing a picture. This might even help you remember the order certain numbers go in.

Start by spending up to a minute studying this list of numbers 1 to 11 - you need to learn the order they're in (left to right, top to bottom). One number occurs twice.

2	10	6	8	4	7
1	3	5	11	9	2

Now cover over the number list and, starting at the first number, join the dots in the order you have learnt. The result will be a simple picture - you'll know if you are **right**.

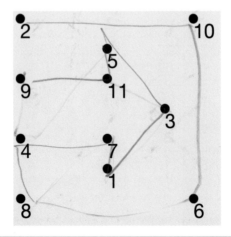

> **Memory Search**

You've probably heard of word searches, but this is a memory search! It works the same way but you have to search your memory for the words.

First of all, spend up to a minute memorising this list of ten materials.

Then cover over the list and see if you can find them all in the word search below - words run in a straight line either horizontally, vertically or diagonally, and may read backwards as well as forwards. No peeking back at the word list!

STRAW	CANVAS	COTTON
GOLD	TWEED	FELT
SILVER	DENIM	LACE
	WOOL	

S	R	W	R	G	N	R	O
I	A	E	A	G	O	A	D
L	O	V	L	R	T	L	N
V	A	D	N	W	T	D	D
E	F	C	E	A	O	S	A
R	S	E	E	N	C	O	S
N	D	I	L	W	I	E	L
T	E	E	W	T	E	M	T

> Kakuro 💡💡💡

Place a digit from 1 to 9 into each empty square to solve the clues.

> Each horizontal run of empty squares adds up to the total above the diagonal line to the left of the run, and each vertical run of empty squares adds up to the total below the diagonal line above the run.

> No digit can be used more than once in any run.

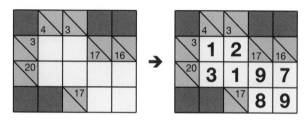

See if you can solve the example above first. Notice how only one possible pair of digits can fit in each of the two-long runs.

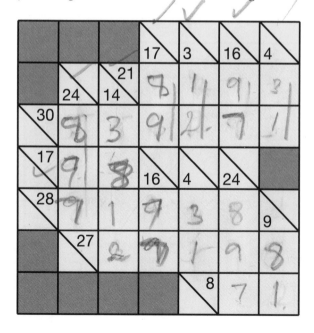

> Sequentially-Thinking

Each of the following sets of numbers follows a different mathematical sequence. By working out what each of these sequences is, can you deduce which number comes next in each case?

5	10	16	23	31	___
2	3	5	7	11	___
25	23	20	16	11	___
1	2	4	8	16	___
243	81	27	9	3	___

> Word Up

Can you pick one letter from the set below to add to each word to make a new word? For example, you could add L to DOE to form DOLE. Each letter is used in only one word.

B	D	E	I	L	L
O	P	T	T	U	U

DRAM	FAVOUR
REACT	TABLE
CLAM	PAPER
PROD	CHAR
POSED	EAGLE
BARD	PEAR

> **Dessert Directions**

Can you draw a path that visits every letter in the grid, spelling out a series of possible items you might eat for dessert? The last letter of each dessert is also the first letter of the following dessert, and you may only move left, right, up or down between letters. Every single letter must be used once and once only in the final path. The start and end of the path are given. Some of the desserts are multiple words (for example 'apple pie' would use two words).

D	R	B	E	T	I	R	A
O	O	S	A	L	L	P	M
U	G	R	I	C	E	P	I
N	H	F	F	E	E	A	S
U	T	O	W	O	D	E	U
I	D	P	N	G	L	D	P
N	D	U	A	U	I	I	S
G	A	T	E	R	F	C	A
P	A	T	I	U	E	L	K
I	O	C	A	N	G	S	E

>> CREATIVITY

> Sliding Around

A good imagination will definitely help you with this puzzle. A pair of scissors and possibly some cardboard and glue/tape are also useful, however!

Start by cutting out the coloured pieces at the bottom of the opposite page. You might want to glue or tape them to a piece of cardboard first to make them more sturdy. Next, place them on the empty board below in the exact arrangement shown at the top of the opposite page. You'll have two pieces left over but they're used in the puzzle on the following page.

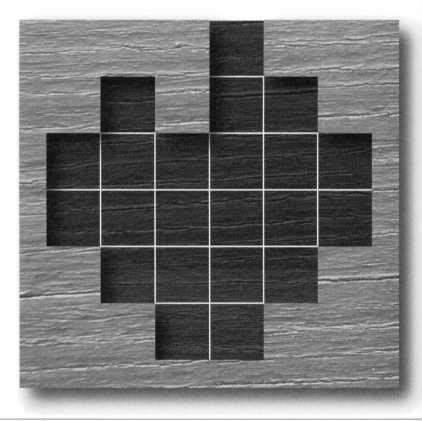

The aim of the task is to work out how to make the red piece, marked with a brown circle, escape from the puzzle board.

The pieces can be moved up, down, left or right (but not diagonally) from square to square, so that the edges remain aligned with the white grid lines.

No two pieces can ever overlap, even during a move, and you cannot rotate or flip over any piece. They must stay in the orientation shown above. Also no piece can stick outside the puzzle board at any time - the only piece that can leave is the red one, and only once it has reached the exit!

See how long it takes you to find the solution - the minimum number of moves from square to square is 31, and this task is not *too* difficult so with a bit of perseverance you should be able to manage it!

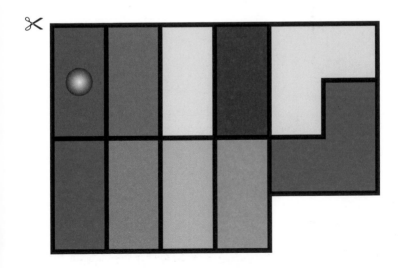

> Sliding Further

Once you've completed (or given up on!) the puzzle on the previous page, try this second one using exactly the same puzzle board and rules, but with a different selection from the pieces you previously cut out:

This area will be cut out
(see previous page)

> Upon Reflection

For each of the three patterns in the left-most column, which of the three options on the right would result if you were to reflect that pattern in the vertical line 'mirror'?

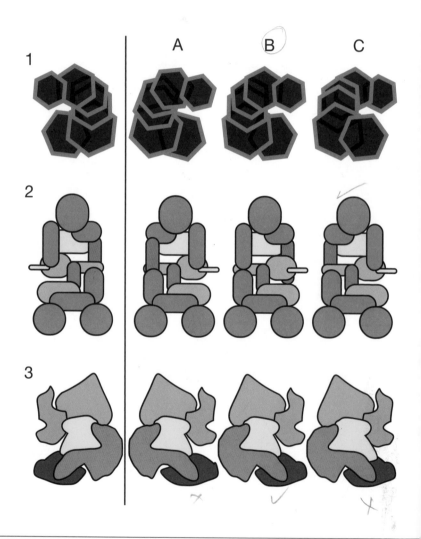

> Cutting Issue

Can you draw exactly three completely straight lines in order to divide this shape into four areas, such that all the areas contain one each of the three different circle sizes and colours?

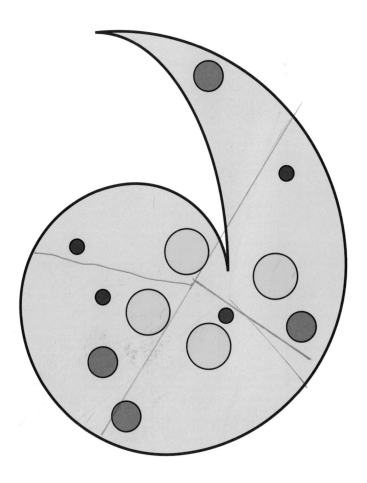

>> REASONING

> Mini Sudoku 💡💡💡

Can you place 1 to 6 into each row, column and bold-lined 2x3 box of these mini Sudoku puzzles?

6		**5**			
4		**6**		**2**	
	5		**3**		**4**
			5		**3**

Did you know that Sudoku was originally created in the US? It was given its name in Japan, but the first puzzles were made by Indiana architect Howard Garns in the 1970s.

	2			**4**	
		1			
3			**6**		
		4			**1**
			2		
	5			**6**	

> Who, What and For How Long?

Can you solve this logic puzzle? The tick-box chart below may help you keep track of your deductions.

Four people have each gone away for trips of differing lengths, and each has engaged in a different activity while gone. Can you work out who did what activity, and how long their trip was?

People:	Karen, Janet, Ian, Harry
Activities:	Cycling, Golfing, Sunbathing, Surfing
Trip lengths:	2 days, 3 days, 5 days, (7 days)

> The total duration of Harry and Janet's trips was equal to the length of Karen's trip.
> The surfer went on a shorter trip than Ian.
> The three-day trip was for golf, and it was not a man who went sunbathing.
> Harry's was not the shortest trip. However, neither of the men stayed seven days.

	Trip length				**Activity**			
	2 days	3 days	5 days	7 days	Cycling	Golfing	Sunbathing	Surfing
Harry	●		●					
Ian		●				●		
Janet	●							
Karen				●				
Cycling				
Golfing				
Sunbathing		●		
Surfing	●			

Person	Trip length	Activity
H.	5	C
?	3	G
?	3	S
k	7	Su B

> Mnemonic Memory

Remembering just the initial letters of words or phrases you wish to recall can sometimes help you memorise longer lists or sentences than you would otherwise find comfortable.

Try this experiment. There are eight vegetables listed here, with initial letters chosen to form two relevant mnemonics. Ordinarily you would then need to also memorise the mnemonics, but they are given below here.

Look at the list for no more than 30 seconds, then cover it over and see how many vegetables you can recall on the empty list beneath.

Cucumber	
Radish	**Y**am
Endive	**A**sparagus
Sweet corn	**M**arrow
Squash	

> Recall the Vegetables

C	
R	Y
E	A
S	M
S	

> Visual Memory 💡💡💡💡

How good do you think your visual memory is? Take a look at the following line of faces for no more than one minute, then cover it over and see how accurately you can redraw the faces on the partially-drawn row below.

Even if you think you find it hard to recall visual details, you can still do this task by focusing on describing to yourself the differences between the pictures and working out what the key details are that you need to remember.

> Recall the Faces

> Circle Lines

Place the numbers 1 to 9 once each into a circle below, so that when complete all of the circles along each line will add up to the total given at the end of that line.

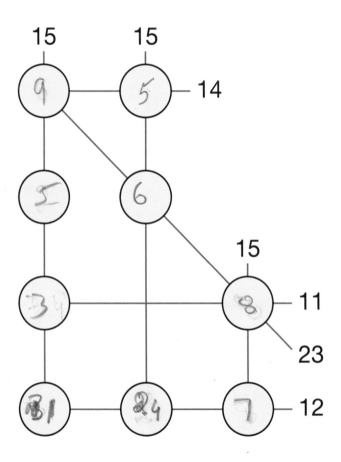

> Brain Chain 💡💡💡💡

How good is your mental arithmetic? See how quickly you can solve each of the following brain chains without making any written notes. Start with the number on the left and follow the arrows while applying each operation in turn. Write the result in the empty box at the end.

32	-50%	÷4	×11	50% of this	**RESULT**
	-16				*22*

46	1/2 of this	-17	+4	×10	**RESULT**
	23				*100*

24	-50%	+9	÷3	×5	**RESULT**
	12				*35*

13	Multiply by four	1/2 of this	+54	÷2	**RESULT**
		26			*40*

40	-3	+59	÷6	+10	**RESULT**
					26

>> WORDS

> Sequence Spotting 💡💡💡💡💡

Can you work out which letter comes next in each of these sequences, and why?

Each sequence corresponds to a real-world ordering, so:

M T W T F __

would be followed by '**S**', since the sequence is days of the week:
Monday **T**uesday **W**ednesday **T**hursday **F**riday and then **S**aturday.

1)	L	V	X	L	C	__
2)	J	F	M	A	M	__
3)	N	U	S	J	M	__
4)	F	S	T	F	F	__
5)	O	Y	G	B	I	__
6)	O	T	T	F	F	__

> Word Chains

By changing only a single letter at each step, and without rearranging the remaining letters, can you travel down from the top to the bottom of each word chain? Each step must contain a regular English word.

For example DOG -> DOT -> COT -> CAT.

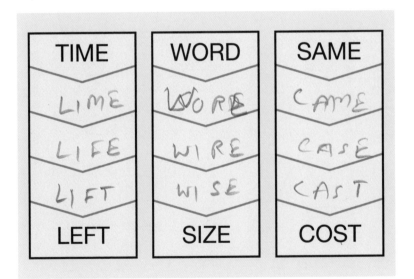

TIME	WORD	SAME
LIME	WORE	CAME
LIFE	WIRE	CASE
LIFT	WISE	CAST
LEFT	SIZE	COST

> Flower Power

The picture below seems to show eight flowers overlapping... but that's not what it really is. There's something else lurking in among the blooms.

What might be hidden? Shade in your choice of areas to reveal a creative image of your own. For example I made the mysterious figure to the right when I tried it out.

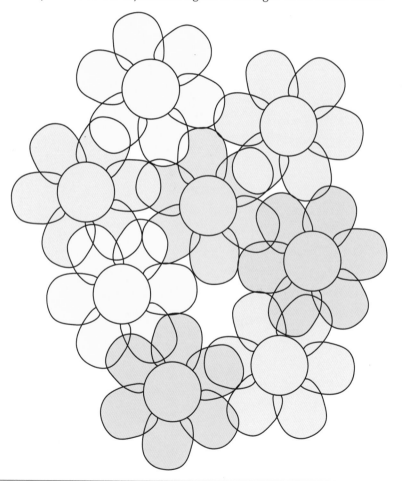

> Cube-ism

In each of the following pictures can you count how many cubes there are? You should assume that all 'hidden' cubes are present.

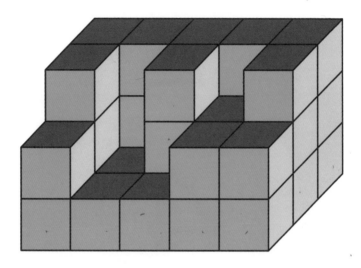

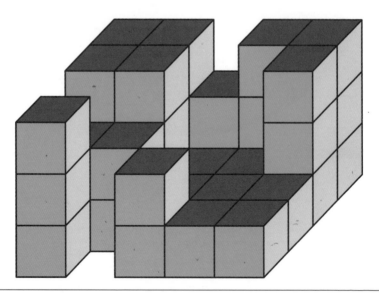

> Mental Shift

Can you rearrange these six pieces in your head, swapping them around in order to reveal a hidden character. Don't rotate or flip over any of the pieces - keep them in their existing orientation.

What character is revealed?

> Skyscraper

Place each number from 1 to 4 into every row and column.

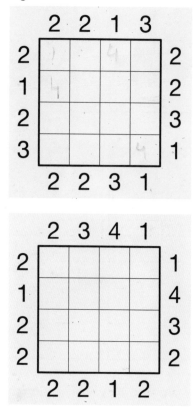

> Each number in the completed grid represents a building of that many storeys. Place the buildings in such a way that each given number outside the grid represents the number of buildings that can be seen from that point, looking only at that number's row or column.

> A building with a higher value always obscures a building with a lower value, while a building with a lower value never obscures a building with a higher value.

> Dominoes

Can you place a full set of dominoes into the grid?
> Draw along the dashed lines to indicate where each domino is placed.
> Use the chart to check off dominoes you've already placed.
> 0 represents a blank on a domino.
> Each domino occurs exactly once in the grid.
One is already placed for you as an example.

2	4	4	3	3	4	4	1
6	2	2	5	1	0	2	4
5	4	2	6	3	0	3	6
6	0	4	1	1	5	0	3
5	6	6	0	1	5	6	2
1	5	2	2	6	1	3	1
0	5	0	4	5	0	3	3

	0	1	2	3	4	5	6	
							✗	0
							✗	1
								2
								3
								4
								5
								6

> Grid Memory

Spend up to a minute studying the shape or shapes you can see through the windows in this grid. Once time is up, cover over the top grid and try to redraw each window as accurately as you can on the empty grid below. Repeating the colours is optional.

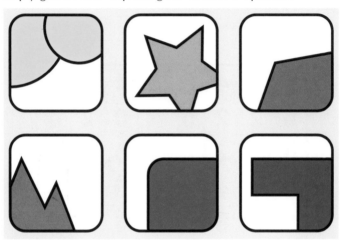

> Windows Dressing

Redraw each window as accurately as you can below:

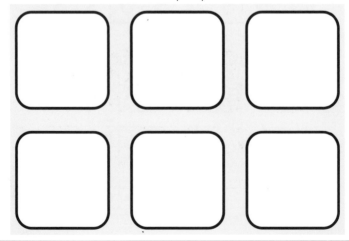

> Which Wall?

Cover over the bottom half of the page and then look at the top arrangement of wallpaper patterns for up to one minute. Once time is up cover over the top half and reveal the bottom half instead. Rotate the book around and follow the instructions below.

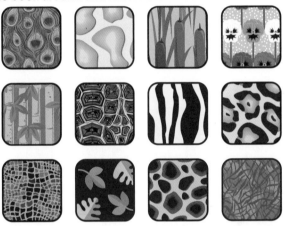

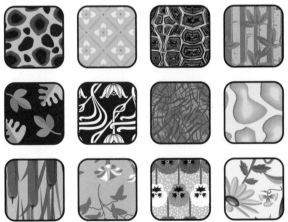

Which of the following patterns are new?

> Recall the Wall

> Calcudoku

Can you place 1 to 5 into each row and column while also obeying the boxed region constraints? The number at the top-left of each boxed region gives the result of applying the given operator between all the numbers in that region. So for example the two boxes in a "3+" region should add to 3, so will contain 1 and 2. If the operator is subtraction or division then start the calculation with the highest value in the box, so for example a region with a 1, 3 and 5 in any order could be a solution to "1-". You can repeat a number within a region, subject to not repeating any numbers in a row or column.

8+			1-	
2÷	3-		3÷	
	0-			20×
3÷		3-		
5+		30×		

Example puzzle

8+ 5	2	1	1- 4	3
2÷ 4	3- 5	2	3+ 3	1
2	0- 3	4	1	20× 5
3÷ 3	1	3- 5	2	4
5+ 1	4	30× 3	5	2

Example solution

8×		8+	1-	
60×	40×			1-
	9+	2÷		
		6×		

> ## Number Pyramid

Can you complete the building of this number pyramid?

Each brick should contain a value equal to the sum of the two blocks directly beneath it.

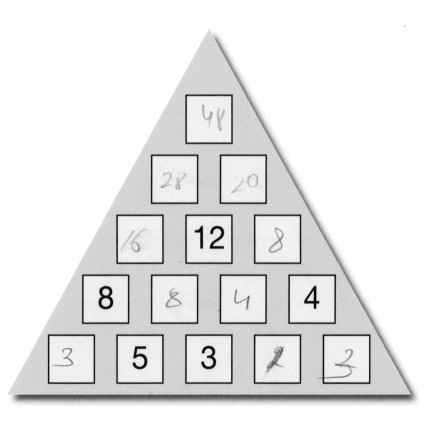

> Word Spinner

By using the centre letter once plus any other selection of letters (also once each only) from the word spinner below, how many regular English words of three or more letters can you find?

Finding 50 is good; 75 is excellent; 100 is unbelievable!

```
        R
    E       O
  N    A   G
    R       I
        S
```

_____

_____

_____

_____

_____

_____

_____

_____

_____

_____

_____

_____

> Pairing Down 🔦🔦🔦

In each of the following sequences, delete one letter from each pair to reveal a hidden word.

For example, in CD BA TX you can delete like this: **CD̶ B̶A T̶X̶** to reveal 'CAT'.

DE LE TE SD ES

MO NK EY SD EN TL EF

GI RA FY FY EL LS

GA RE TH IS NE AR

> A Little Too Close

What unusual interpretation can you give to each of these images?

The top-left one might be hills... but perhaps it is a two-humped camel from slightly behind? Write under each picture what it is.

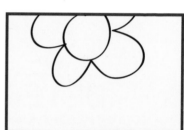

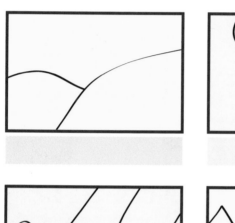

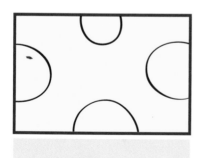

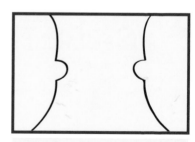

> Missing Around

There are two of each of the images in this collection below, except for one of them which is an odd one out. Can you find this image? Images may be rotated but none of them are reflected.

> Triangle Tangle

This image is packed full of triangles.

By drawing over existing lines only, can you find 24 different triangles?

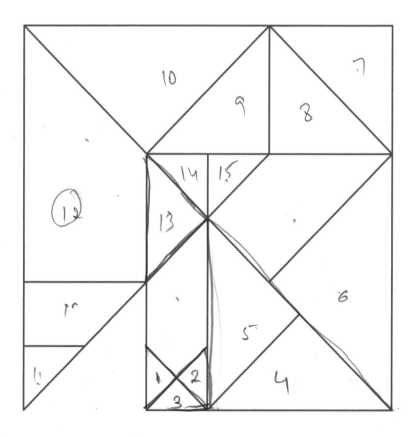

> King's Journey

Can you find a sequential path through the grid?

> Find a route from 1 to 81 by moving only as a king moves in chess: left, right, up, down or diagonally from square to adjacent square.
> You must visit every square, and the given numbers must occur at that number square in the journey. So for example square '25' must be the 25th square in the path.

31	32	34	35	43	44	48	49	50
30	33	36	42	45	47	54	53	51
27	29	37	41	46	60	59	55	52
26	28	38	40	61	62	66	58	56
3	25	24	39	63	65	67	71	57
4	2	1	23	64	68	70	73	72
5	11	13	14	22	69	76	75	74
6	10	12	15	18	21	77	78	81
7	9	9	16	17	19	20	80	79

> Bridges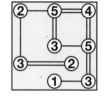

Join circled numbers with horizontal or vertical lines, such that each number has as many lines connected to it as specified by its value.

> No lines may cross, and no more than two lines may join any pair of numbers.

> The finished layout must allow you to travel from any number to any other number just by following one or more lines.

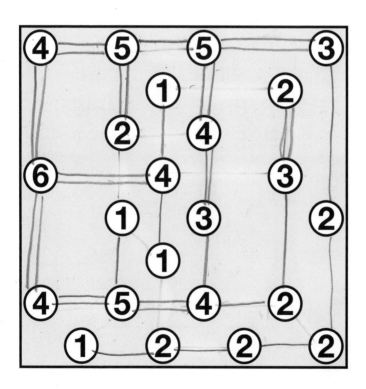

> Crossed Words 💡💡💡

Cover over the bottom half of this page first. Next, spend up to one minute trying to memorise the following list, which mainly consists of pets.

When time is up, cover the word list and uncover the bottom half. Place the words you can remember into the grid, fitting them as in a crossword puzzle so they share letters where they cross. By using this grid to prompt you with word lengths and these crossing letters, can you remember all of the words and complete the puzzle?

DOG	MOUSE
GERBIL	EYESIGHT
GUINEA PIG	GIRL
HAMSTER	IMPISH
HORSE	PET

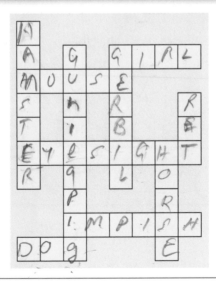

> ## Shaping up your Memory

Study the grid of shapes to the right for no more than one minute, then cover it over and see how accurately you can recall the shapes and their positions on the grid below.

The arrangement of the shapes follows various patterns, so by looking for these patterns you can reduce the amount you need to remember.

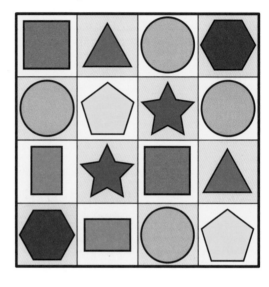

If you have some coloured pens handy then feel free to try remembering the colour of each shape too, or you could try this as a separate second memory task.

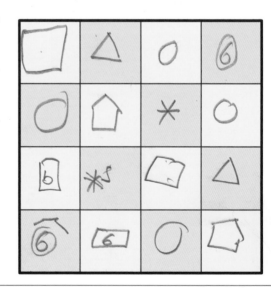

> **Sum Square** 💡💡

Can you place all of the numbers 1 to 9 once each into the empty squares in this puzzle, such that each of the given numbers results when reading across each row and down each column respectively.

Calculate values step by step as if typing into a calculator, not following rules of mathematical precedence.

3	×	6	÷	9	=	2
×		−		+		
2	×	4	×	8	=	64
−		×		+		
1	×	5	+	7	=	12
=		=		=		
5		10		24		

> ## Shopping Conundrum

I go shopping and buy the following items:

Item	Cost	Item	Cost
Cheese	3.50	Tea	4.20
Strawberries	4.50	Toothpaste	3.75
Apples	3.20	Coffee	7.25
Oranges	4.95	Sugar	3.33
Bread	2.64	Butter	1.37

> If I round each item to the nearest whole number (e.g. 3.20 to 3, or 4.50 to 5), what is the total of these rounded values?

> What is the exact difference between this estimate and the amount I actually spent?

> How much change did I get from a 50.00 note?

> If I had 1000.00, how many times could I make the exact same shop above?

> Vowel Play

In each of the following words all of the vowels have been deleted.

Can you work out what each of the original words was?

SHMP

STST

TLRT

TPTP

QTNS

> Flying Letters

By picking in order one letter from the outer orbit, one letter from the middle orbit and then one letter from the inner-most orbit, how many three letter English words can you find? For example, 'AIM'. There are at least 20 more to find.

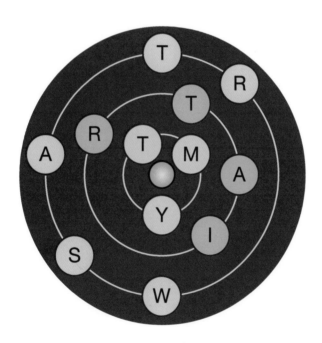

> Fridge Magnets

Imagine rearranging the fridge magnets below. What interesting sentences and phrases can you come up with? Write them on the freezer cabinet below! You can use each word multiple times.

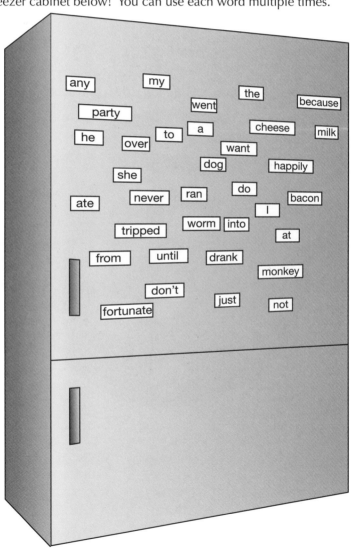

> Private Roads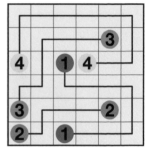

Can you connect each pair of identical numbers together using only horizontal and vertical lines from square to square? Only one line can enter any square, so in other words the lines can't touch or cross.

Take a look at the example solution on the right to be sure you understand the rules.

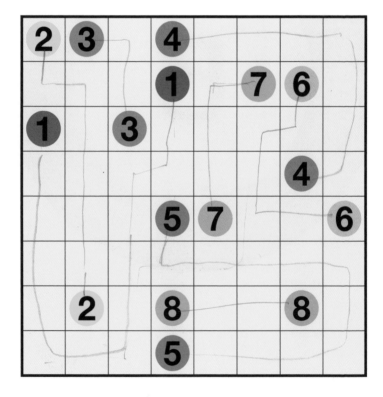

> **Four Piece Arrangement**

By drawing along the existing lines, can you divide this shape up into four identical pieces, with no pieces left over? The pieces may be rotated versions of one another but you cannot flip or 'turn over' any of the pieces.

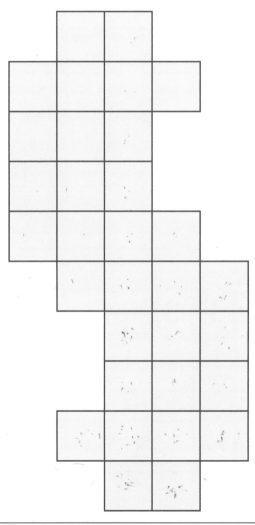

>> REASONING

> Wraparound Sudoku

Place 1 to 5 into each row, column and bold-lined jigsaw region.

Some regions 'wrap around' the outside of the puzzle, travelling off one end of a row/column and continuing on the square at the opposite end of the same row/column.

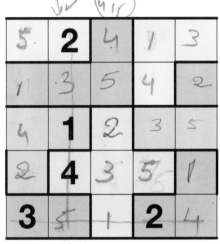

> Three by Four

Can you fill each of the tetromino pieces in the grid below with one of the three following symbols so that no two tetrominoes containing the same piece touch on any of their sides? Two are already filled to get you started.

> Order Some Vegetables

How good are you at remembering what order some objects are in?

Start by covering over the bottom half of the page, then study the order of the vegetables in the row below for up to one minute. Once time is up, cover over the top of the page and reveal the bottom half. Try to number the corresponding fruits on the bottom set to show the order they were in originally, so for example write '1' under the vegetable that was first, and so on.

> Remember the Order

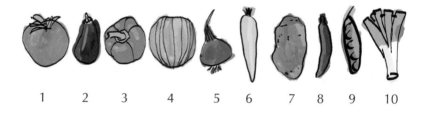

1   2   3   4   5   6   7   8   9   10

> Recall the Order

5   6   3   8⁄4   1   7   10   8   2   9

> ## Colour by Memory

Spend up to a minute studying the pattern of colours in the top grid. Once time is up, cover over the top grid and try to either colour in or label each box in the bottom grid with the same colour as in the top grid.

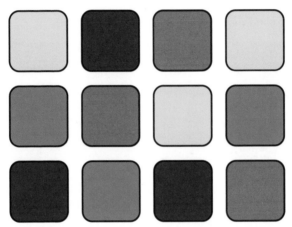

> ## Colour Me In

Shade or label each window with its original colour:

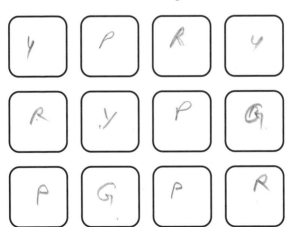

> ### Kakuro

Place a digit from 1 to 9 into each empty square to solve the clues.
> Each horizontal run of empty squares adds up to the total above the diagonal line to the left of the run, and each vertical run of empty squares adds up to the total below the diagonal line above the run.
> No digit can be used more than once in any run.

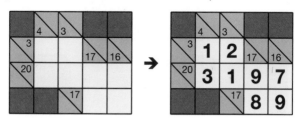

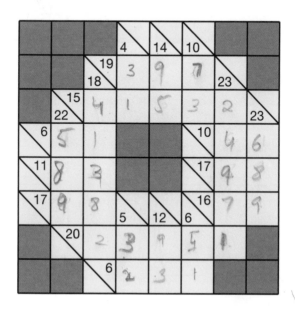

> Number Darts

By choosing exactly one number from each ring of this dartboard, can you find three segments whose values add up to each of the listed totals?

For example, to reach a total of 99 you would take 38 from the outer ring, 38 from the middle ring and 23 from the inner ring.

70

79

97

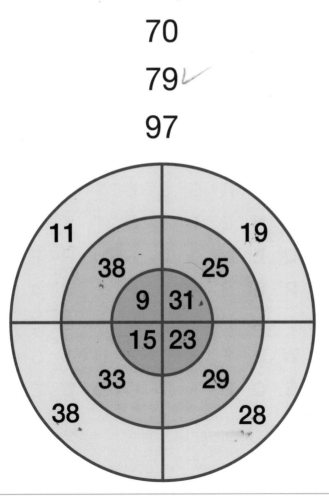

>> WORDS

> Bird Spotting

Can you find all of the listed birds that can be found at wetlands flying somewhere in the grid? Since they are flying, the words are in one of the following patterns:

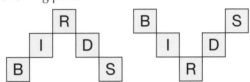

CRAKE	GOOSE	OUZEL	STINT
DIVER	GREBE	PIPIT	STORK
EGRET	HERON	QUAIL	SWIFT
EIDER	HOBBY	SCAUP	TWITE

> ## Sort it out

You'd think it was pretty easy to sort a set of words into alphabetical order, but it can be a little trickier when this conflicts with another existing ordering!

> How quickly can you sort these numbers into alphabetical order of their written form?

1 2 3 4 5 6 7 8 9 10 15 25

One Two, Thre

> How long does it take you to order these days in reverse alphabetical order?

Monday	Tuesday
Wednesday	Thursday
Friday	Saturday

> Can you sort these months into alphabetical order, ignoring their first letter? So for sort order July would be 'uly', for example.

January	February
April	May
March	December
June	August

> My Rhyming Ain't No Crime-ing

Our brains enjoy the patterns in poetry, which is why this art form is elevated above the more prosaic - quite literally. Poetry is generally based on metre and rhythm, but rhyming can also be an important feature of many poems. It's also used for the punch line in many jokes, since a witty rhyme strikes us as both amusing *and* clever, and seems to somehow just 'fit'.

For each of the following phrases, see if you can come up with a rhyming second phrase. This can be serious or amusing (or a mix) as you please, but the more creative the better! As an example, the first line could be rhymed with "An urging for a cup of tea!".

1)
The light of dawn awakes in me,

_____

2)
The sound of silence fills the air,

_____

3)
The tumbleweed goes tumbling by,

_____

4)
Wondrous words I'd scribe one day,

_____

> Something to Reflect Upon

Can you reflect all of the lines in this image in the vertical dashed-line 'mirror'? The grid of dots is provided for reference.

If you complete this task successfully then you will reveal a stylised image.

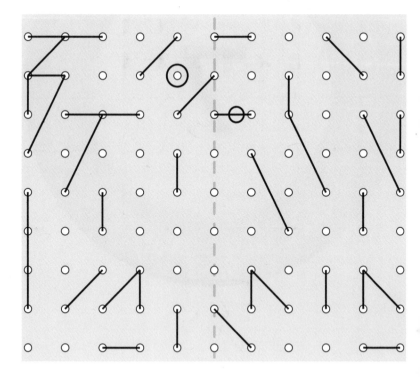

> Layer by Layer

What is the minimum selection of patterns, 1 to 8, which you can overlay in order to form the composite image at the bottom? If there is more than one way of making the pattern then you must find the minimal set (the smallest number of patterns required).

You may not rotate or reflect the patterns, and there must be no 'extra' lines in the result compared to the target image.

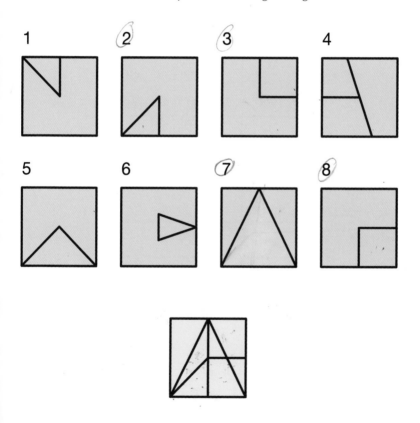

>> REASONING

> Inequality Sudoku

> Place 1 to 6 into each row, and column, plus each bold-lined 2x3 box, while obeying the inequality signs.

> Less than ("<") and greater than (">") signs between some squares indicate that the values in these two squares must be greater than or less than one another as indicated by the sign. The sign always points towards the smaller number.

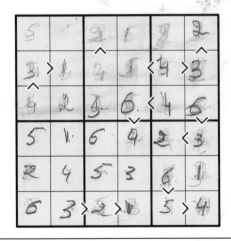

> Light-Up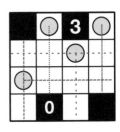

Place light bulbs in empty squares so that all of
the empty squares in the puzzle either contain a
bulb or are at lit up by at least one bulb.

> Light bulbs illuminate all squares in the same
  row and column up to the first black square
  encountered in each direction. -

> No light bulb may illuminate any other light bulb, although empty
  squares may be lit by more than one bulb.

> Some black squares contain numbers - these numbers indicate
  how many light bulbs are placed in the neighbouring squares
  immediately adjacent above, below, to the right and left of these
  black squares.

> Not all light bulbs are necessarily clued via black squares.

> Homes, Sweet Homes

It's time to practise using your visual memory again.

Study the three houses in the picture below for no more than one minute, then cover them over and redraw them as accurately as you can on the house outlines below.

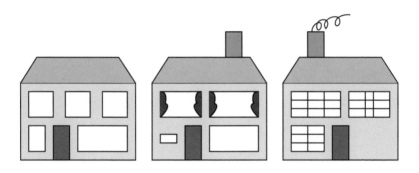

> Remember Your Homes

How accurately can you redraw the three houses? There's no need to bother with the colours unless you want to.

> In for the Long Haul

Virtually all of the memory tasks in this book work on your short-term memory, but challenging your long-term memory is also very important.

There are many techniques which can be used to make it easier to remember facts over extended periods of time. For example, attaching strong emotions to them through ridiculous associations works well, since our brains are primed to remember what happens at 'critical' points - or those where we have these strong emotions in other words. Attaching ridiculous imagery also helps, because it is remarkable enough to make us really take note and therefore remember. Whatever techniques you choose to use, if any, try to learn the following facts over the next few minutes. There's a workout on recalling them in four weeks.

> Puzzle Power

Riddles and puzzles have existed as long as humanity. They are found in religious writings from before 1,000BC, and the famous Riddle of the Sphinx appears in Sophocles' play *Oedipus Tyrannus* first performed in around 430BC.

The age of modern puzzles began with the invention of the crossword by Arthur Wynne, whose *Word-Cross* puzzle was first published in US paper *New York World* in 1913, before making its way to the UK in 1924 courtesy of the *Sunday Express*.

In late 2004 another sea change in puzzles began when *Sudoku* was brought to Western attention by *The Times* of London. Soon the logic puzzle appeared in newspapers and magazines across the world. Its phenomenal appeal encouraged many publications to try out other previously obscure "Japanese" puzzles, such as the number crossword *Kakuro*. Ironically both Sudoku and Kakuro actually have their origin in the US, but were named and refined in Japan.

> Number Anagram

Given the following set of numbers and mathematical signs, can you rearrange them in order to obtain each of the given results?

You must use all of the numbers and signs, but you can use as many additional 'brackets' as you like - for example: (4x5)-(2x3)=14.

2	3	5	7	25
+	−	×	×	

Result: 100

Result: 166

> Age Awareness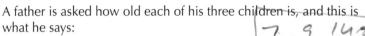

A father is asked how old each of his three children is, and this is what he says:

> **The combined age of all of my children is 24**

> **Bradley is two years older than Andrew**

> **Two years from now, Charlie will be twice Andrew's age**

Can you work out how old each of his three children is?

> Sporting Soup

Can you rearrange the soup of floating letters below to spell out the names of four sports? Each letter should be used exactly once in the resulting set.

> Back to Back

Each of the following word middles can have an identical letter inserted both before and after to make a word. For example, _IGH_ can have 'S' added to make 'SIGHS', or 'T' added to make 'TIGHT'.

Can you find all of the possible solutions for each of the word middles below? The number of solutions to look for is given in each case. None of the words is obscure, although a couple are informal terms.

3 words: **_ASHE_**

4 words: **_EA_**

6 words: **_I_**

3 words: **_AS_**

3 words: **_INGE_**

2 words: **_OU_**

3 words: **_RO_**

> Sliding Around

Start by cutting out the coloured pieces at the bottom of the opposite page. You might want to glue or tape them to a piece of cardboard first to make them more sturdy. Next, place them on the empty board below in the exact arrangement shown at the top of the opposite page. You'll have one piece left over but it's used in the puzzle on the following page.

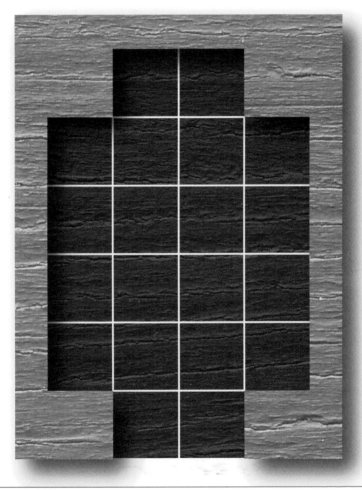

The aim of the task is to work out how to make the red piece, marked with a brown circle, escape from the puzzle board.

The pieces can be moved up, down, left or right (but not diagonally) from square to square, so that the edges remain aligned with the white grid lines.

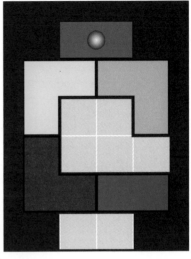

No two pieces can ever overlap, even during a move, and you cannot rotate or flip over any piece. They must stay in the orientation shown above. Also no piece can stick outside the puzzle board at any time - the only piece that can leave is the red one, and only once it has reached the exit!

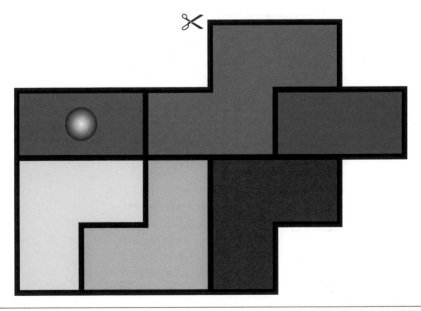

> Sliding Further

Once you've completed
(or given up on!) the
puzzle on the previous
page, try this second one
using exactly the same
puzzle board and rules,
but with a different
selection from the pieces
you previously cut out.

This area will be cut out
(see previous page)

> Pattern Pairings

Each of the following patterns occurs twice, so can you match each pattern with its identical partner? The patterns are rotated with respect to one another, but none of them are reflected or manipulated in any other way.

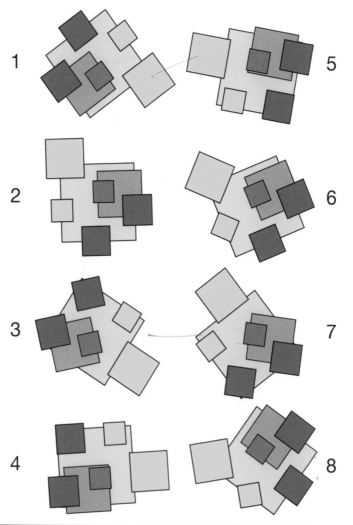

> Cut Out Cubes

All except two of the following shapes can be cut out and folded along the lines to form a six-sided cube.

Which are the odd ones out that won't form a complete cube?

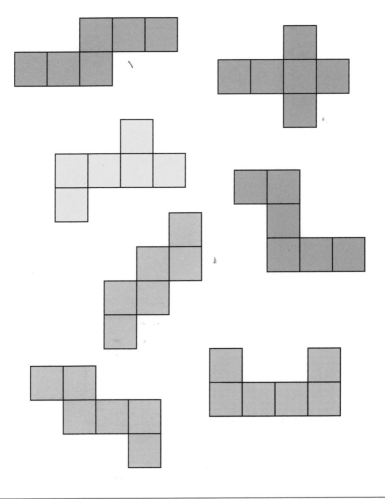

> Sudoku-8

The most common Sudoku are 9x9, but the puzzle works almost as well at 8x8 with the benefit of being a little bit easier too! Can you place 1 to 8 into each row, column and bold-lined 4x2 box?

		5			7		
	2					5	
4			7	6			5
		8	5	7	4		
		3	1	5	6		
8			4	1			7
	8					1	
		4			3		

			3	5			
	2		8	4		6	
		5			6		
4	6					3	7
7	5					8	6
		4			1		
	3		5	6		2	
			4	3			

> Card Box

Can you place each of the four following cards into the 2x2 grid, with one card per box?

Place the cards so that:

> The red cards are on the same row.
> The value of both cards in one of the columns sum to the value of one of the cards in the other column.
> In both columns a lower-value card is at the bottom.
> The top row increases in value as you read from left to right.

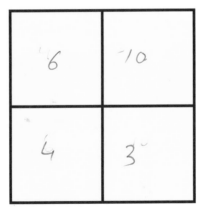

>> MEMORY

> Memory Search

To try this Memory Search, first spend no more than one minute memorising this list of ten Commonwealth countries.

Then cover over the list and see if you can find them all in the word search below - words run in a straight line either horizontally, vertically or diagonally, and may read backwards as well as forwards. No peeking back at the word list!

CANADA	INDIA	SINGAPORE
CYPRUS	NAMIBIA	TONGA
GHANA	PAKISTAN	ZAMBIA
	SEYCHELLES	

> Fruit Feast 💡💡💡

First of all cover over the bottom half of the page. Next, study the collection of fruit immediately below for no more than one minute.

When time is up, cover over the top half of the page and reveal the bottom of the page. Can you work out exactly which fruits have been eaten? You will need to rotate the book first.

Can you work out which fruits have gone missing between the previous arrangement and this one?

> Fruit's Up

> Calcudoku

Can you place 1 to 6 into each row and column while also obeying the boxed region constraints? The number at the top-left of each boxed region gives the result of applying the given operator between all the numbers in that region. So for example the two boxes in a "3+" region should add to 3, so will contain 1 and 2. If the operator is subtraction or division then start the calculation with the highest value in the box, so for example a region with a 1, 3 and 5 in any order could be a solution to "1-". You can repeat a number within a region, subject to not repeating any numbers in a row or column.

7+ 5	8+ 1	10+ 4	6	5+ 3	2
2	4	3	19+ 1	6	5
1- 2	1- 5	6	3	4	3× 1
1	576× 6	4	3- 2	5	3
4	3	2	10× 5	1	24× 6
5÷	5	2÷		2	4

> ## Balloon Numbers

In each of the following cases, which of this set of balloon numbers should you burst in order to leave a group of balloons that add up to the given total?

For example, to obtain a total of 19 you would burst all except the 7 and the 12 balloons.

Total: 28   7 17 4

Total: 44   32 12

Total: 41   7 12 22

Total: 50   7 4 22 17

> Feeling Stumped?

Can you fit all of the trees listed below into this grid? Write one letter per square as in a crossword.

All of the listed trees must be used at least once, but some of them will be needed more than once. It is up to you to work out which ones!

Happy planting!

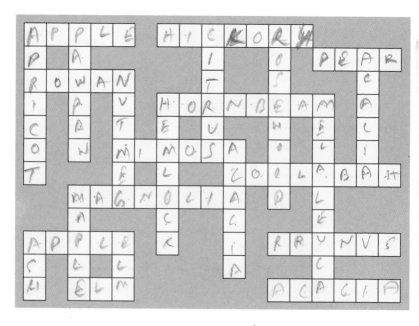

ACACIA	HEMLOCK	NUTMEG
APPLE	HICKORY	PAWPAW
APRICOT	HORNBEAM	PEAR
ASH	MAGNOLIA	PRUNUS
CITRUS	MAPLE	ROSEWOOD
COOLABAH	MELALEUCA	ROWAN
ELM	MIMOSA	

> **Making-up Words**

Can you rearrange the fragments on each line into the correct order to spell out a word? For example "MP SA LE" could be rearranged for "SAMPLE".

TE NT IGE IN LL

TE SI LA AS MI

SC AL DE NT TR AN EN

ON SC ATI FU OB

IC OB RO AU PH ST CL

> And the Rocks Cried Out

Lots of brightly-coloured pebbles have washed up on the beach below. But what beast from the depths of the ocean has also washed up along with them? By joining pebbles together with either curved or straight lines as you please, what can you reveal?

If you're feeling uninspired then why not start with random lines, then take a step back to see what the result looks like so far and take it from there.

> Driftwood

Next time you're on a beach you can try this task for real! Look for an area with pebbles, find a suitable stick and scratch some lines in the sand. Of course, there's nothing stopping you doing this in muddy ground somewhere too...

> Egg-cellent Puzzle

Can you work out which two of the following egg halves will join back together to form a perfect complete egg? You won't need to flip any of them over in order to do this.

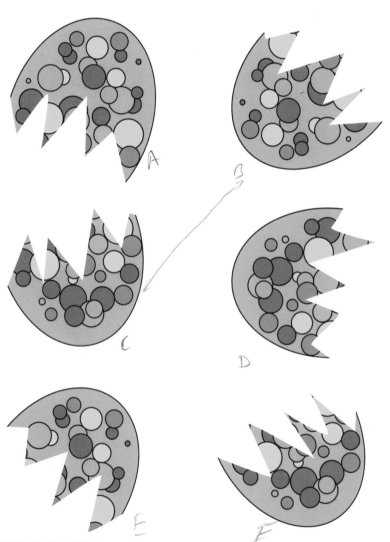

> Mix It Up

When you mix paints you end up with different colours.

Without trying it out first, can you work out what colour will result when mixing each of the following combinations of the three primary paint colours?

>> REASONING

> Slitherlink

One of the most pure logic puzzles ever invented, Slitherlink asks one simple question: can you draw a single loop that passes by each digit the stated number of times?

3	1	1	2	3	3
2	2		0		2
	3		0		2
3		0		3	
3		0		2	3
3	1	2	2	1	1

Try the example puzzle above - the solution is given on the right so you can be sure you understand the rules. You can only join dots with horizontal or vertical lines, and the loop cannot cross or overlap itself at any point. Note how each number has the given count of adjacent line segments.

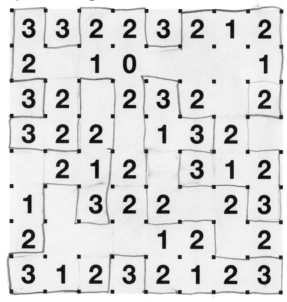

> Logical Inference

Given the first two examples below, what is the most probable transformation being applied to the two patterns on the left-hand side to produce the two patterns on the right-hand side?

If you apply this same transformation to the third pattern, which of the three options a, b or c should replace the question mark?

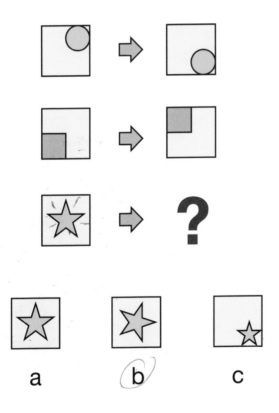

> The Un-ugly Duckling

How good is your memory for written detail? Read the following short passage, then cover over the top half of the page and read the second version of it below. Can you underline all of the words that have been changed?

There once was a beautiful, yellow duckling. He was very proud of his gorgeous, fluffy feathers. Even when it rained, the water bounced off his back like splashes off a human's umbrella. His little orange feet waddled him from A to B, and he lived happily forever on his lake.

> Spot the Duck-erence

Highlight the changed words:

There once was a gorgeous, yellow duckling. He was very proud of his beautiful, fluffy feathers. Even when it poured, the rain splashed off his back like water off a human's umbrella. His little ducky feet paddled him from A to Z, and he lived happily forever on his pond.

> Spin the Memories

This is an interesting test of your visual memory because it requires you to both recall and manipulate an image simultaneously.

Firstly study the top image for no more than one minute, then cover it over and try to redraw it on the grid below. But there's a twist - literally. When you redraw it you must rotate the entire image through 90 degrees clockwise, as shown by the arrow. A few elements are given to help you along the way. Don't just rotate the book!

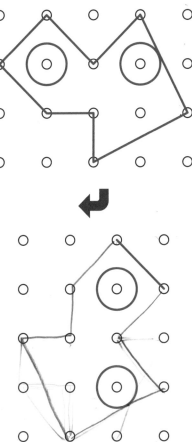

> Brain Chain

How good is your mental arithmetic? See how quickly you can solve each of the following brain chains without making any written notes. Start with the number on the left and follow the arrows while applying each operation in turn. Write the result in the empty box at the end.

| 71 | -47 | Multiply by three | One half of this | 75% of this | RESULT 27 |

| 18 | Fifty percent of this | ×4 | Square root of this | ×12 | RESULT 72 |

| 55 | 4/5 of this | 75% of this | +64 | -60 | RESULT 37 |

| 30 | 1/2 of this | +34 | √ | +65 | RESULT 72 |

| 98 | ÷2 | +3 | 25% of this | +92 | RESULT 105 |

> Fenced In

Sara is building a fence around a rectangular plot of land 3m by 2m in shape.

> If she puts up a fence along just one 3m side of the plot of land, and each rectangular section of fencing is 1m wide and requires a fence post at both ends, how many fence posts does she need?

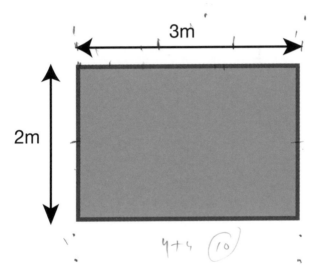

3m

2m

4 + 4 (10)

> If Sara now fences off the entire perimeter of this land, how many fence posts will she have used in total for the whole 10m fence?

> If in addition to the 1m-wide fence sections Sara had also bought some 2m wide fence sections, what is the minimum number of fence posts she would need now?

6

> Word Spinner

By using the centre letter once plus any other selection of letters (also once each only) from the word spinner below, how many regular English words of three or more letters can you find?

Finding 15 is good; 24 is excellent; 30 is unbelievable!

TONNE TONE   Ten, Tie Tin

Tint, mic net NOT

cot, into, cent

tit, Tot con tic

e Note, oint nite

coir

```
        I
    O       N
  N    T    C
    N       T
        E
```

> Cryptographic Conundrum

Can you decode the four quotes that are encoded on this page?

Each quote is encoded with a (different) constant letter rotation around the alphabet, so for example A might be replaced with B, B with C, C with D and so on through to Z being replaced with A.

Dcan iwdht lwd spgt id upxa vgtpian rpc tktg prwxtkt vgtpian.

Gdqtgi U Ztcctsn

Twsmlq ak ljmlz, sfv ljmlz ak twsmlq

Bgzf Cwslk

Dro qbokdob dro ylcdkmvo, dro wybo qvybi sx yfobmywsxq sd.

Wyvsobo

Fq fp kbsbo qll ixqb ql yb texq vlr jfdeq exsb ybbk.

Dblodb Biflq

> Initial Thoughts

If each of the following acronyms actually existed, what do you think they might stand for in the given context?

As an example, **OVS** could be "**O**ver-enthusiastic **V**olunteer **S**yndrome" in the charity industry.

T A C
(Television industry)

U F F
(Food industry)

W S P
(Fashion industry)

> Circuit Breaker

A piece is missing from this electronic circuit. Can you pick which one of the four pieces below fits into the gap in order to complete the circuit? Once complete all of the lines will connect at both ends. You may need to rotate the correct piece.

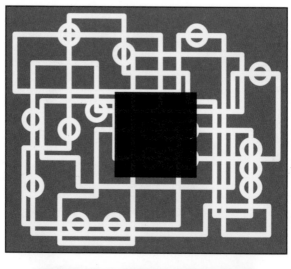

> Ten-Four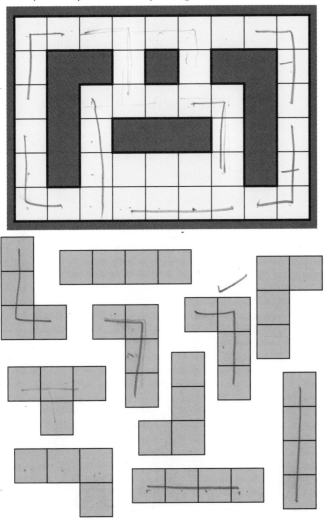

Can you place all of the tetrominoes (the orange four-square pieces) into the pattern at the top, so as to cover every empty square? You may use each tetromino once each only, and you may **not** rotate or flip over any of the pieces when placing then.

> Solo Battleships

You've probably played the classic two-player pencil and paper game, but did you know that you can also play Battleships in a solo version?

> Locate the listed set of hidden ships of various lengths in the grid.
> Each ship can be placed horizontally or vertically only, and cannot touch another ship horizontally or vertically (diagonally is okay).
> Numbers next to each row or column specify the number of filled ship segments in that row/column.

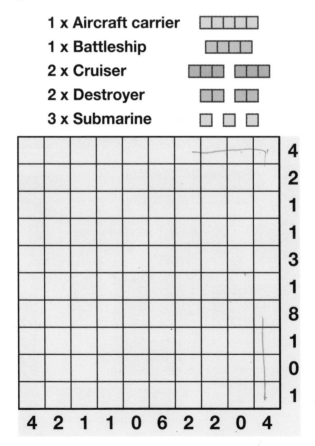

1 x Aircraft carrier

1 x Battleship

2 x Cruiser

2 x Destroyer

3 x Submarine

> As Easy As A, B, C

Can you fit the letters A, B and C exactly once each into every diagonal row in this grid?

> Letters in the purple areas indicate which letter appears closest to that end of the row. For example, an 'A' is the first letter found when following the row down and right from the 'A' at the top of the puzzle.
> Some squares (two per row) will be empty.

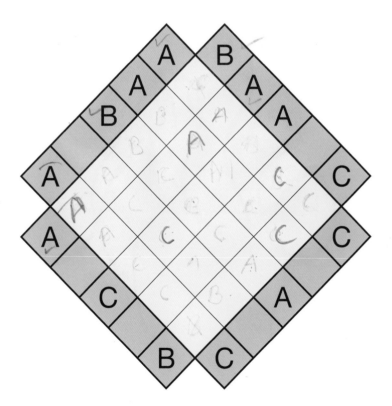

> Pump up the Balloons

How good is your visual memory? Study the balloons below for about 10 seconds, then spin the book around quickly through 180 degrees (a half revolution) and read the instructions above the picture on the opposite page.

> Inflated Picture

Without looking at the opposite page, which of this set of balloons were in the original picture, in the same location? Tick or mark them in some way so you can check your answer.

> Ballooning Fun

Don't read the **bold** questions below yet. First, study the image on this page for as long as you like, then cover it up and answer the questions:

> **How many balloons are in the picture?**
> **Which colour of balloon occurs the most?**
> **Which colours occur only once in the image?**

> Number Paths

By moving up, down, left or right from square to touching square, can you find a path that is 10 squares long and where each square is equal to the previous square "+4"? So you could move from "11" to "15" in the right-most column, for example, because 11 + 4 = 15.

31	27	23	19	21
29	25	21	17	11
33	39	43	13	15
37	41	19	15	19
49	45	21	25	29

Once you've found the "+4" path, what is the length of the longest path you can find by moving from square to square applying "-2"? This time you may move to diagonally-adjacent squares too.

> Got Bottle

You have 3 water containers, each of a different size. Container A can hold 3 litres, container B can hold 5 litres and container C can hold 8 litres.

If containers A and B are both empty but container C is filled to the brim with 8 litres of water, how can you now pour this water from one container to another so as to end up with exactly 4 litres of water in both B and C? (Doing it 'by eye' is not the solution! There is a mathematically precise method to find.)

You may find the series of empty jars helpful when solving.

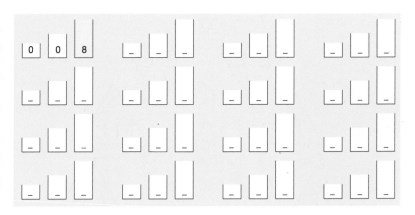

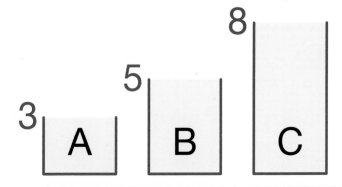

> Fitting Letters

Can you place each of these triangular jigsaw pieces into the empty pyramid in order to spell out a word reading across each row? There are therefore six words in total.

Each piece is used once and they may not be rotated or reflected - place them in exactly the same orientation they are shown.

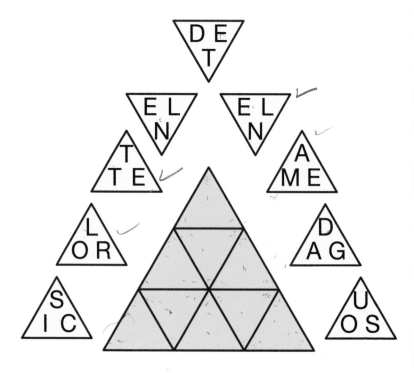

> Word Slider 💡💡💡💡💡

The picture below shows a 'word slider'. By moving each of the five sliders up and down, you can spell words out through the window in the middle.

Simply by imagining moving the sliders up and down, how many regular English words of five letters can you spell out? One word is spelled out for you already. There are **over 20** others to discover.

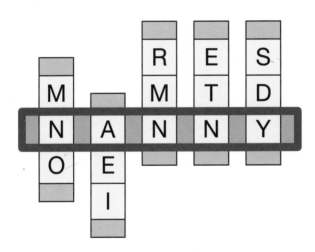

> Colourful Circle Creation Challenge

Ideally you'll need coloured pens for this creativity challenge!

It's time to release your artistic side by colouring in the areas in the image below to reveal... whatever you like. Design a wallpaper pattern, liberate a hidden creature or simply colour it in as the will takes you. Whatever you do, you'll be being creative!

The title of your creation:

> A Question of Perspective

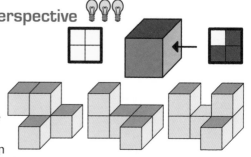

Each of the three pink cube arrangements, when viewed from the direction of the arrow, has the same profile. If you were to shade in the left-hand cream grid to represent this profile then the result would be the grid at top-right. For both of the following cube arrangements, what would their profiles look like if viewed from the same side-on direction? Shade in their cream grids.

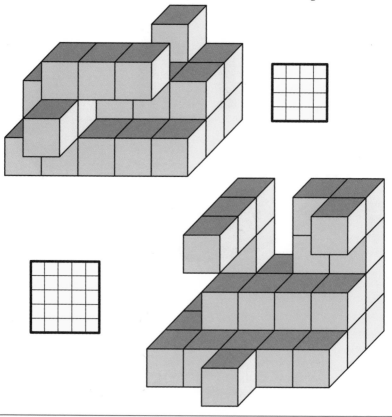

> Speed Counting

For each of the questions below, write an estimate in the first column as quickly as you can. Then once you have done all of the estimates go back and count more precisely. How good was your gut instinct?

How many faces have...	Estimate	Actual
Blue or brown eyes	18	13
A red or yellow nose	3	4
An eye patch	3	2
Symmetrical eyebrows		
Smiling or unhappy mouths	5	10
Red eyes **and** a yellow nose	2	2

> Jigsaw Sudoku

It's surprising how a small change can really make you think about Sudoku all over again. In these two puzzles, can you place 1 to 5 into each row, column and bold-lined jigsaw shape?

2	4	3	1	5
5	1	2	3	4
1	3	4	5	2
4	5	1	2	3
3	2	5	4	1

2	3	4	5	1
5	1	3	4	2
4	2	1	3	5
3	5	2	1	4
1	4	5	2	3

> Hanjie

Shade in squares in the grid to reveal a picture while obeying the clue constraints at the start of each row or column.

> The clues provide, in order from the left or the top, a list of the length of every run of consecutive shaded squares in each row or column.

> Multiple runs in a row/column are separated by at least one empty square. For example "2,3" means there is a run of 2 shaded squares, followed by at least one empty square, and then 3 consecutive shaded squares.

> Take a look at the example above to see how the clues correspond with the solution.

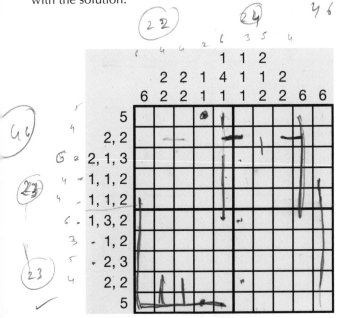

Clue: Timely decoration?

> Grid Memory

Spend up to a minute studying the pattern of shapes in the top grid. Once time is up, cover over the top grid and try to redraw each window as accurately as you can on the empty grid below. Repeating the colours is optional.

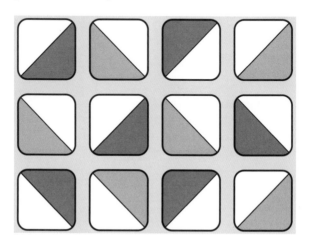

> What's in the Windows?

Redraw each window as accurately as you can below:

> Out for the Long Haul

In order to do this task you need to have previously completed the memory workout 'In for the Long Haul' on page 91. Please follow the instructions there before reading the questions below.

> Riddling Recall

It's time to find out just how much you remember! The answers to all of the following questions are given in the original text.

> Who wrote the play *Oedipus Tyrannus,* and around what year was that play first performed?

> What famous riddle does the play feature?

> Who is credited with the invention of the crossword?

> What name did the inventor originally give the puzzle?

> In what year and US newspaper was the crossword first published?

> And in what newspaper did the crossword first appear in the UK?

> What year saw the introduction of Sudoku by *The Times* of London?

> In which country do the "Japanese" puzzles Sudoku and Kakuro actually have their origin?

> Kakuro

Place a digit from 1 to 9 into each empty square to solve the clues.

> Each horizontal run of empty squares adds up to the total above the diagonal line to the left of the run, and each vertical run of empty squares adds up to the total below the diagonal line above the run.

> No digit can be used more than once in any run.

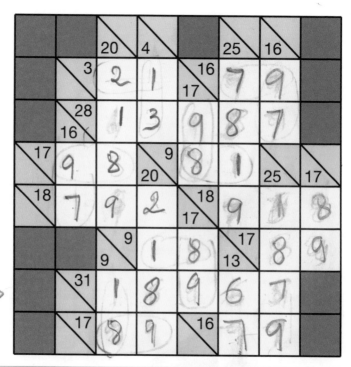

> Number Buddies

For each set of numbers, can you join them into pairs that each obey the given relationship? For example, 3 and 6 obey the relationship "×2". Each number is used exactly once.

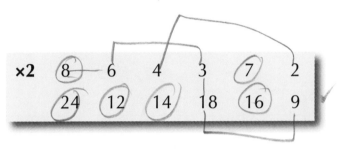

×2   8 — 6   4   3   7   2
24   12   14   18   16   9

+7   18   11   31   10   8   15
17   4   25   24   12   5

÷3   9   12   15   81   27   6
36   2   54   5   3   18

> Floral Path

Can you draw a path that visits every letter in the grid, spelling out a series of flowers? The last letter of each flower is also the first letter of the following flower, and you may only move left, right, up or down between letters. Every single letter must be used once and once only in the final path. The start and end of the path are given.

A	C	A	C	W	E	E	E	A
A	N	S	I	S	S	T	P	L
P	L	I	A	M	I	L	E	L
D	L	Y	R	A	E	W	D	I
R	A	L	E	A	S	T	E	U
O	G	A	Z	A	I	E	S	M
N	A	R	C	I	N	R	O	A
N	S	U	S	S	U	T	L	L
O	W	D	R	O	P	E	O	W

> ## Letter Trail 💡💡💡💡

How many words of three or more letters can you find by starting on any square in this grid and moving from square to touching square, either right/left/up/down or diagonally, spelling out a word? You cannot use any square more than once in a single word. For example, 'CARD' is okay; 'DAD' is not allowed.

Finding 15 is good; 20 is excellent; 25 is unbelievable!

C	R	A
O	C	D
N	O	I

(handwritten annotations)

Okra

ocar aCra Rado
Acid acco acordian
ramcid Accord Noor

air

Craon Raid
Car
Road
Cord
Noad

Drain

Coin dia
doc

corn, cod, con, Aid Rod
Rod Racoon, corn
Acorn Accord, Dov
Ram, acra

> A Little Too Close

What unusual interpretation can you give to each of these images?

The top-left one might be a wheel... but perhaps it is a snail crawling past, or the back of a bee? Write under each picture what it is.

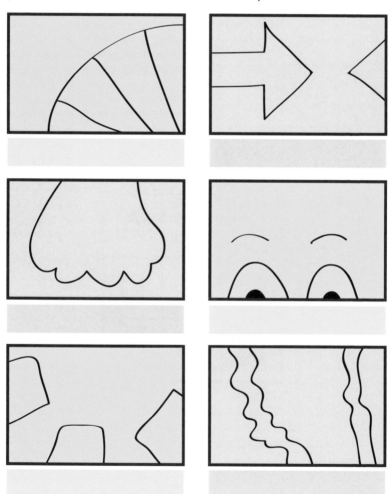

> Cutting Edge

Can you draw exactly three completely straight lines in order to divide this shape into four areas, such that all the areas contain one each of the three different circle sizes and colours?

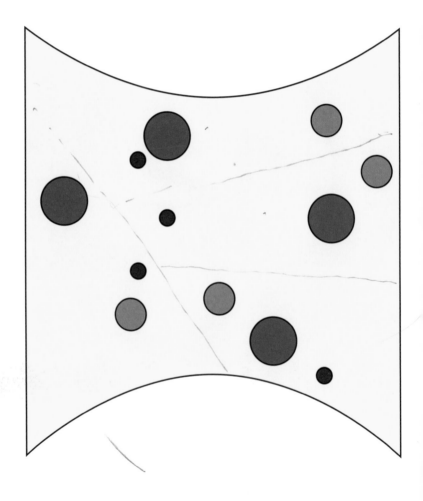

> Locksmith

This key only matches one of the lock profiles beneath. Which one?

> Skyscraper

Place each number from 1 to 5 into every row and column.

> Each number in the completed grid represents a building of that many storeys. Place the buildings in such a way that each given number outside the grid represents the number of buildings that can be seen from that point, looking only at that number's row or column.

> A building with a higher value always obscures a building with a lower value, while a building with a lower value never obscures a building with a higher value.

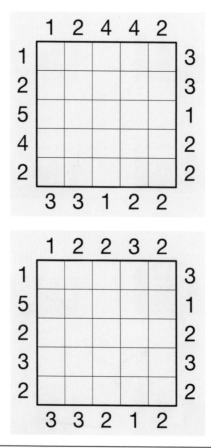

> Set Phrase-rs to Stun 💡💡💡

Can you work out which phrase each of these pictures is hiding?

For example, "GAit's allME" could be "It's all in the game".

2 your
your
your boots
your

U something S

> Stick To It

How good is your memory for visual detail?

Spend no more than one minute trying to remember the appearance of each of these stick people.

Once time is up, cover over the top images and try to redraw them as accurately as you can on the heads given below.

> It's All In Your Head

Now redraw them:

> Healthy Swap Shop 💡💡💡💡

Cover over the bottom half of the page before looking at the following arrangement of fruit and vegetables for no more than one minute. Once time is up cover over the top half of the page instead. Can you say which fruit and vegetables are new to the mix, and which ones are now missing? You will need to rotate the book first.

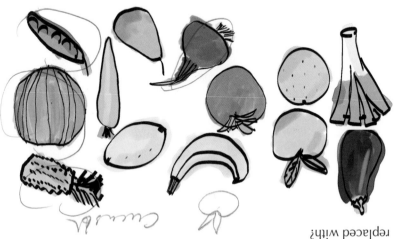

> 4 Fruit or Veg

Which fruit or vegetables are missing, and what have they been replaced with?

> ### > Sum Square

Can you place all of the numbers 1 to 9 once each into the empty squares in this puzzle, such that each of the given numbers results when reading across each row and down each column respectively.

Calculate values step by step as if typing into a calculator, not following rules of mathematical precedence.

4	×	2	×	1	=	8
+		+		×		
5	−	3	×	8	=	16
×		×		×		
9	−	7	×	6	=	12
=		=		=		
81		35		48		

$\theta D M 95$

> Killer Sudoku

Killer Sudoku is regular Sudoku with an added killer twist!

Not only do you need to place 1 to 6 into each row, column and 3x2 bold-lined box, but you must also place numbers so that they add up to the total given at the top-left of each dashed-line cage. You also can **not** repeat a number within a dashed-line cage (this restriction actually makes the puzzle easier, not harder, because it eliminates some possibilities).

9			11			9		
1	5	3	6	2	4
9	3	9			5
4	2	6	1	3	5
5	1	2	13		
			4	6	3
13			10	6	3
3	6	4	2	5	1
8	8				
6	4	5	3	1	2
2	3	1	15		
			5	4	6

> **Mixed-up Words**

In each of the following sentences, find an anagram of the CAPITALISED word that will fit into the gap.

> He needed to RESHIP the fruit before it began to _____.

> In what SECTOR of the shop would she find a _____?

> The steady clip-clop of the CART-HORSE sounded to its owner like the finest _____.

> Observing the latest UPTREND, it was _____ to buy.

> He tried to play the _____, but all he heard was a strange GROAN.

> It took some effort to get ORGANISED, but it was the most _____ event.

> To finalise the settlement, the SENORITA needed to _____ the documents.

> Word Relationships

By deducing the relationship between the first pair of words, can you work out the word that completes each sentence?

1: DOG is to PUPPY as CAT is to...

> LION   TIGER   KITTEN   TOMCAT

2: BOOK is to SHELF as FRUIT is to...

> BOWL   CUP   SUN   VEGETABLE

3: CHAIR is to SIT as TELEVISION is to...

> RECORD   FURNITURE   RELAX   WATCH

4: RUNG is to LADDER as BULB is to...

> GARDEN   THERMOMETER   LAMP   CAR

5: OAR is to BOAT as PADDLE is to...

> CREEK   STEAMER   VOYAGE   WATER

> Sorry, WHAT'S in the box?!

Draw in the boxes to show what you think is inside them!

> Pyramid Puzzle

If you were to cut out and fold up this shape net, which of the triangular pyramids below would result?

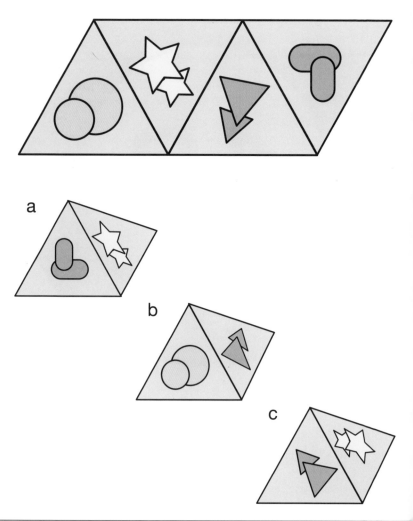

> Combined Approach 💡💡💡

Mentally try to combine the two images below, so the white squares on one are replaced with the contents of the coloured squares from the other, and vice-versa.

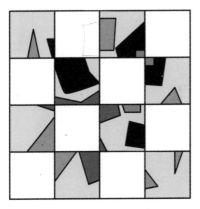

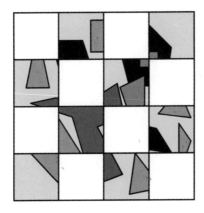

> How many blue shapes can you count? *6*
> How many four-sided shapes are there?
> How many triangular shapes can you count?

> Hitori 💡💡💡

Shade in squares so that no number occurs more than once per row or column.

> Shaded squares cannot touch in either a horizontal or vertical direction.

> All unshaded squares must form a single continuous area

2	5	6	2	4	6
1	6	5	4	6	3
3	3	1	2	2	5
3	1	4	5	6	2
5	4	2	1	3	1
6	4	6	3	6	5

You may find it helpful to circle numbers you know are definitely *not* shaded.

1	3	4	4	6	5	6
5	1	3	6	3	2	4
1	7	2	4	3	4	7
5	4	5	1	5	7	5
3	7	6	4	7	4	2
7	5	4	2	1	6	3
6	5	1	1	4	3	2

> King's Journey

Can you find a sequential path through the grid?

> Find a route from 1 to 81 by moving only as a king moves in chess:
  left, right, up, down or diagonally from square to adjacent square.
> You must visit every square, and the given numbers must occur
  at that number square in the journey. So for example square '25'
  must be the 25th square in the path.

17	**18**	24	**25**	27	28	29	30	**31**
16	**19**	23	26	73	72	35	34	32
15	20	**22**	76	**75**	**74**	71	36	**33**
13	14	21	77	79	**81**	70	**68**	37
11	12	**8**	7	**78**	**80**	**69**	67	**38**
10	9	**3**	**1**	6	**64**	65	66	39
53	**55**	2	4	5	63	**62**	61	40
52	54	56	**57**	58	**59**	60	44	41
51	50	49	48	**47**	46	45	**43**	42

> Mnemonic Memory

Remembering just the initial letters of words or phrases you wish to recall can sometimes help you memorise longer lists or sentences than you would otherwise find comfortable.

See if you can use this technique to remember the list of 11 fruits given here. Take no more than a minute to study the list. A suggested fruity mnemonic is provided: APPLE TOMATO.

When time is up see if you can recall all of the words on the page opposite.

Apricot

Peach

Plum

Lemon

Elderberry

Tomato

Orange

Melon

Avocado

Tangerine

Olive

> Mnemonic Recall

Instructions for this task are on the opposite page.

Cover over the left-hand page and use the top half of this page to see if you can recall all 11 fruits:

A	T
P	O
P	M
L	A
E	T
	O

> Long-term Memory

Mnemonics can be very powerful. In fact, you might even recall the list of fruit this time tomorrow if you are prompted with the mnemonic. So bookmark or otherwise make a note of this page, then come back in 24 hours or so and see if you can recall all (or any) of the fruit given the mnemonic below:

A	T
P	O
P	M
L	A
E	T
	O

> Square Dance

Looking at this 3×3 grid, how many squares of all sizes (1×1, 2×2 etc) can you count in total?

(handwritten notes): 14
1×1 = 9
2×2 = 4
3×3 = 1

And how many squares of all sizes can you count in this 4×4 grid?

(handwritten notes): 16
1×
30

What about in this 5×5 grid? How many squares can you count?

(handwritten notes): 25
2×2 = 16
3×3 = 9
4×4 = 4

Can you work out a general method of calculating the number of squares in a grid of any size 'x by x'?

> Calcudoku

Can you place 1 to 6 into each row and column while also obeying the boxed region constraints? The number at the top-left of each boxed region gives the result of applying the given operator between all the numbers in that region. So for example the two boxes in a "3+" region should add to 3, so will contain 1 and 2. If the operator is subtraction or division then start the calculation with the highest value in the box, so for example a region with a 1, 3 and 5 in any order could be a solution to "1-". You can repeat a number within a region, subject to not repeating any numbers in a row or column.

24×		9+			30×
1–			2÷		
15+		3–		3÷	
		3÷		16×	
5+	12×		120×		
				15×	

> Word Up

Can you pick one letter from the set below to add to each word to make a new word? For example, you could add L to DOE to form DOLE. Each letter is used in only one word.

C D H O O P
P R T T T Y

PARED	FOND
DRAGON	RUST
BARNET	GRATE
IRATE	ROUGHS
EARL	TRUST
READ	LOUD

> Word Chains

Please see page 47 for instructions.

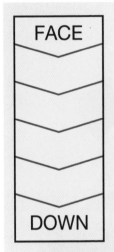 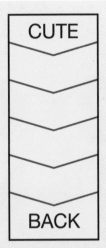 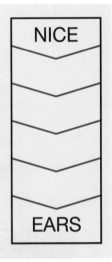

| FACE | CUTE | NICE |
| DOWN | BACK | EARS |

This pattern is not part of the word chains workout but is the reverse of the creative challenge on the following page!

> Some Reassembly Required

Start by cutting out the square pattern at the bottom of the page, and then cutting along the black lines. You should end up with 8 pieces. Next try to work out how to make each of the following shapes with them - the first is easiest! You can rotate or turn over pieces, but not overlap them. Then try to come up with some of your own too!

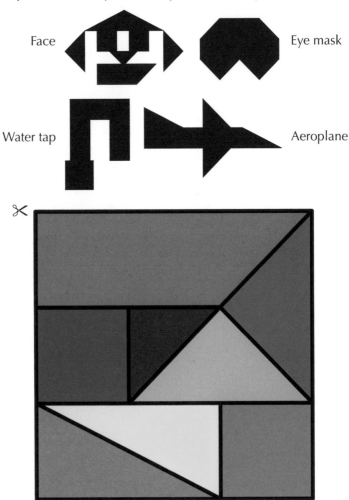

Face

Eye mask

Water tap

Aeroplane

> Cube-ism

In each of the following pictures can you count how many cubes there are? You should assume that all 'hidden' cubes are present.

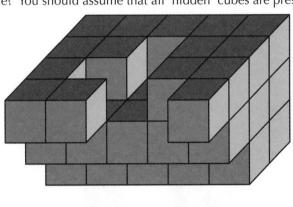

> It's all in the Detail 💡💡💡

By studying the top picture, can you work out where each of the five zoomed-in details below appears in that picture? None of them are rotated, but they're all enlarged.

> Futoshiki

Place 1 to 6 into each row and column of these two puzzles. You must also place each number so that every inequality sign is obeyed - in other words, each pair of squares with an arrow in-between should have the arrow pointing to the lower of the two numbers.

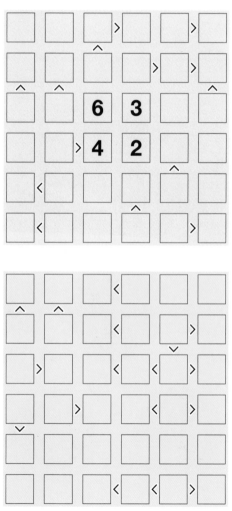

> Slitherlink

Draw a single loop by connecting together the dots so that each numbered square has the specified number of adjacent line segments.

> Dots can only be joined by horizontal or vertical lines.
> The loop cannot touch, cross or overlap itself in any way.

```
3 1 1 2 3 3
2 2   0   2
    3   0   2
3     0   3
3     0   2 3
3 1 2 2 1 1
```

```
  2     3     3     3
  2     2     2     2
2   3 1 2 2 2
2 2 3 1           2
2           1 3 1 1
  2 1 1 0 2     2
3   2   2   2
2   2   2   2
```

> Memory Search

To try this Memory Search, first spend no more than one minute memorising this list of twelve card games.

Then cover over the list and see if you can find them all in the word search below - words run in a straight line either horizontally, vertically or diagonally, and may read backwards as well as forwards. No peeking back at the word list!

WHIST	SOLO	SWITCH
BRIDGE	BRAG	POKER
TRUMPS	SNAP	PATIENCE
SEVENS	PIQUET	BLACKJACK

N	K	B	C	E	E	G	T	M	P
O	S	P	M	U	R	T	S	W	O
P	B	L	A	C	K	J	A	C	K
P	I	R	E	T	R	O	S	S	E
S	A	Q	I	N	I	E	V	S	R
W	W	N	U	D	V	E	W	U	V
R	H	S	S	E	G	I	N	O	A
C	P	I	N	B	T	E	L	C	W
C	I	S	S	C	T	O	S	C	E
R	L	S	H	T	S	B	R	A	G

> Remember the Difference

Cover over the bottom half of this page and then study the country road scene to the right for no more than 30 seconds. Then cover over the top half of the page instead, and rotate the book around to follow the upside-down instructions below.

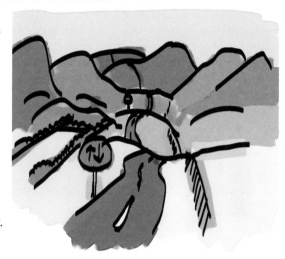

> Recall the Difference

There are six differences between this image and the one you have just remembered.

Can you spot them all?

If you can't, try memorising this image instead and then flipping back to the original to see if you can spot them there.

>> NUMBERS

> Kakuro

Place a digit from 1 to 9 into each empty square to solve the clues.
> Each horizontal run of empty squares adds up to the total above the diagonal line to the left of the run, and each vertical run of empty squares adds up to the total below the diagonal line above the run.
> No digit can be used more than once in any run.

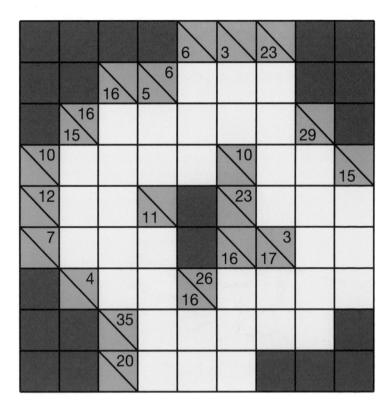

> ## Calorie Counting

One day I keep track of the calorie count in what I eat:

Breakfast		Dinner	
Cereal	420	Baked potato	275
Milk	100	Chicken	175
		Sauce	150
Lunch		Side dishes	180
Bread	250		
Sandwich meat	200	**Snacks**	
Dressing	120	Nuts	225
Salad	25	Fruit	80

> How many calories have I eaten that day?

> Assuming I burn 75 calories per mile walked, how many miles would I need to walk in order to have retained a "net" intake of 2000 calories?

> If I wanted to reduce dinner to 585 calories, what percentage of my meal should I eat? You should assume I eat equal percentages of all items in the meal.

> If I had cut my use of dressings and sauces in half, plus eaten only two-fifths of each of my snack servings, how many calories less would I have consumed that day?

> Phase Faze

Each of these pairs of clues solves to a pair of words that are homophones - so they sound the same but are spelt differently, such as CEDAR and SEEDER.

1a) Weapons   **1b) Charitable donations**

2a) Not the finished thing   **2b) Cool air current**

3a) Control or limit   **3b) Edge of pavement**

4a) Percussion instrument   **4b) A mark standing for something**

5a) Civic ruler   **5b) Female horse**

6a) Filled   **6b) Formal agreement**

7a) Great power   **7b) Tiny arachnid**

8a) A young branch   **8b) Sloping channel**

> Intertwined 💡💡💡

Two words of the same length have got mixed up together on each of the following lines, but the letters have remained in the same order. Can you disentangle them and work out what the two original words were? In each case the words are also related to one another in some way.

For example, DCOGAT contains the words 'DOG' and 'CAT'.

TSENQNUAISHS

CPAORRTATOOT

TCARIMPEROAD

RSADHIINAINNTG

> Sliding Around

Start by cutting out the coloured pieces on the right of the opposite page. You might want to glue or tape them to a piece of cardboard first to make them more sturdy.

Next, place them on the empty board below in the exact arrangement shown on the bottom-left of the opposite page. You'll have one piece left over but it's used in the puzzle on the following page.

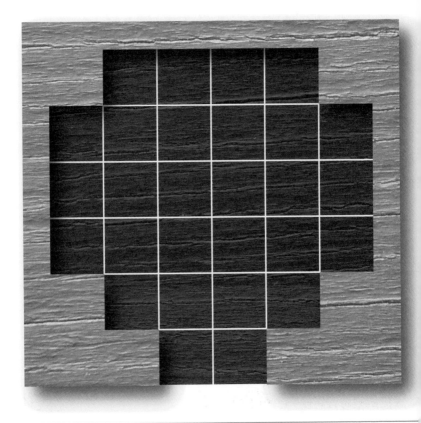

The aim of the task is to work out how to make the red piece, marked with a brown circle, escape from the puzzle board.

The pieces can be moved up, down, left or right (but not diagonally) from square to square, so that the edges remain aligned with the white grid lines.

No two pieces can ever overlap, even during a move, and you cannot rotate or flip over any piece. They must stay in the orientation shown below. Also no piece can stick outside the puzzle board at any time - the only piece that can leave is the red one, and only once it has reached the exit!

There's a second puzzle on the page overleaf too.

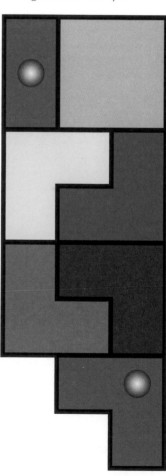

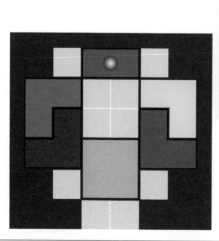

>> CREATIVITY

> Sliding Further

Once you've completed (or given up on!) the puzzle on the previous page, try this second one using exactly the same puzzle board and rules, but with a different selection from the pieces you previously cut out.

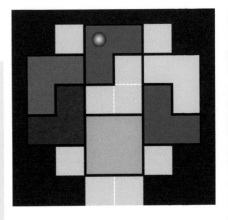

This area will be cut out
(see previous page)

These two puzzles are fairly tricky, but they can certainly be done! The first one takes a minimum of 30 moves to complete.

> Private Roads

Can you connect each pair of identical numbers together using only horizontal and vertical lines from square to square? Only one line can enter any square, so in other words the lines can't touch or cross.

Take a look at the example solution on the right to be sure you understand the rules.

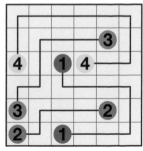

> Mental Manipulation 💡💡💡

How good is your mental manipulation? See if you can answer the following questions entirely 'in your head', without making any drawings or trying anything out with real objects!

> A cube has six faces, but how many edges does it have? And how many corners does it have?

> If I put a cube down on a solid table, what is the maximum number of edges I can see at any one time without moving my head?

> How many faces does a square-based pyramid have?

> If you placed two identical cubes together so that they touched perfectly face-to-face, without any part sticking out anywhere, how many faces could you count on the resulting joined object?

> Imagine a three-dimensional letter 'T', made out of two identical touching cuboids fused together. How many faces are there on this object?

> Bridges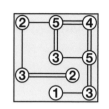

Join circled numbers with horizontal or vertical lines, such that each number has as many lines connected to it as specified by its value.

> No lines may cross, and no more than two lines may join any pair of numbers.

> The finished layout must allow you to travel from any number to any other number just by following one or more lines.

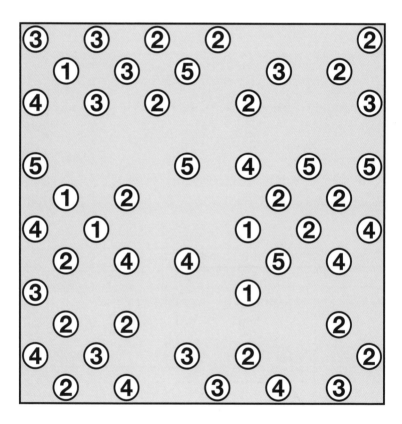

> Jigsaw Sudoku

You might have already tried the 5x5 Jigsaw Sudoku puzzles in week 11, so in which case you should be ready for these 6x6 ones. Can you place 1 to 6 into each row, column and bold-lined jigsaw shape?

> Joined-up Memory

If you've tried the previous "Joined-up Memory" task then you'll know what's in store here. In this particular workout you'll try to memorise some numbers, but you'll know how you're doing and maybe get a few hints as you also reveal a picture.

Start by spending up to a minute studying this list of numbers 1 to 13 - you need to learn the order they're in (left to right, top to bottom). The first number occurs twice since it is also the last number.

3	7	14	5	2	6	8	
12	4	9	1	10	11	13	3

Now cover over the number list and, starting at the first number, join the dots in the order you have learnt. The result will be a simple picture - you'll be **twice as sure you're correct** as last time.

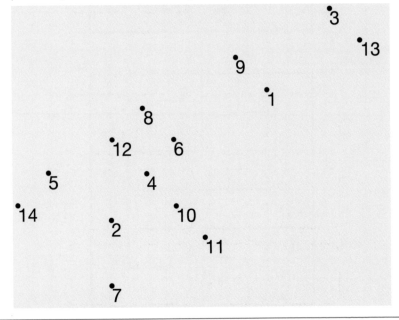

> Colour by Memory

Spend up to a minute studying the pattern of colours in the top grid. Once time is up, cover over the top grid and try to either colour in or label each box in the bottom grid with the same colour as in the top grid.

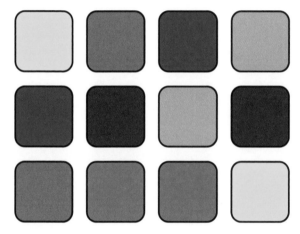

> Colour Me In

Shade or label each window with its original colour:

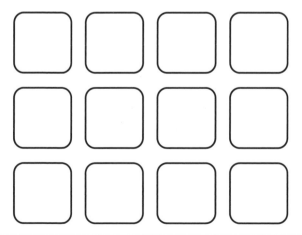

> Sequentially-Thinking

Each of the following sets of numbers follows a different mathematical sequence. By working out what each of these sequences is, can you deduce which number comes next in each case?

1	2	2	4	8	32	___
2	3	5	8	12	17	___
123	115	108	102	97	93	___
16	19	24	31	40	51	___
576	288	144	72	36	18	___
2	5	10	17	26	37	___

> Number Darts

By choosing exactly one number from each ring of this dartboard, can you find three segments whose values add up to each of the listed totals?

For example, to reach a total of 35 you would take 10 from the outer ring, 10 from the middle ring and 15 from the inner ring.

65

75

85

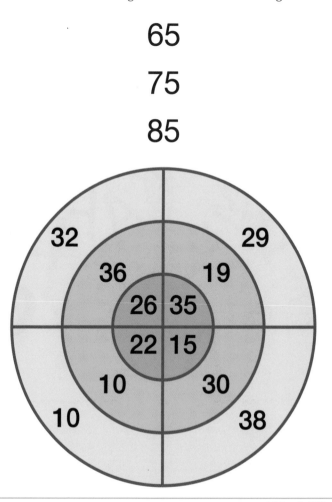

> Floating Furniture

Can you rearrange the floating letters below to spell out the names of various pieces of furniture? Each letter should be used exactly once in the resulting set.

> **Thinking Alike**

For each of these groups of words can you draw lines to join them into pairs? Each word can be in only one pair, and the two words in each pair must share a common meaning. All words are used.

RELISH	**SAUCE**
ENDURING	**FIXED**
MARKED	**CONSTANT**
NOTED	**CHEEK**
ENJOY	**CORRECTED**

WONDER	**THINK**
FOLLOW	**EMULATE**
FLOURISH	**MIRROR**
REFLECT	**GENIUS**
SUCCEED	**PROSPER**

> All Alone in the Night

Imagine a quiet shack on a hill side surrounded only by open fields. A roaring fire burning in the hearth, and the muffled sound of snow flakes falling gently onto the roof. You step outside and see the evening sky decorated with hundreds of brilliant white snow flakes.

Take a picture of that scene in your mind, then fill in the gaps - what else is hidden in the sky that night? Join the snow flakes together in the scene below with either straight or curved lines to reveal what else is floating in the sky.

> Mental Shift

Can you rearrange these nine pieces in your head, swapping them around in order to reveal two hidden characters. Don't rotate or flip over any of the pieces - keep them in their existing orientation.

What is revealed?

> Pattern Problem

The white squares in the grid below have been filled in by following a consistent rule. By applying the same rule again, can you deduce what should go in the square marked with a question mark in order to complete the grid?

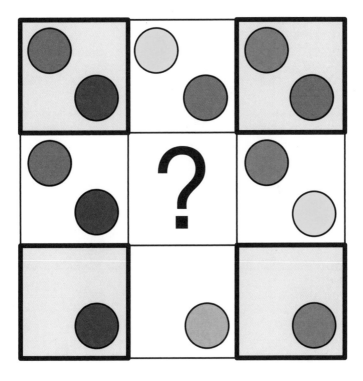

> Rectangles

Draw solid lines along the dashed lines in order to divide the grid up into a set of rectangles.

> The number inside each rectangle must be equal to the number of dashed-line squares it contains.

> Each rectangle must have exactly one number inside it.

	5							
	2	3						2
			4			16		
			2					
9	7	2	2				2	3
				6				3
		2			2	9		
		6						
			5					
						8		

> Find the Truth

Can you work out who is telling the truth here?

A Fizzing Fantasia has gone missing from Ye Olde Sweete Shoppe. Three boys were spotted leaving the sweet shop shortly afterwards so are questioned as to who stole the sweet.

Two of the boys tell the truth while the third answers with a lie.

Pete:	It wasn't me who stole the Fizzing Fantasia.
Dan:	I saw Simon take it.
Simon:	Pete is the guilty one.

Using your powers of logical deduction, deduce which one of the boys took the sweets.

> Grid Memory

Spend up to a minute studying the patterns in each window in the top grid. Once time is up, cover over the top grid and try to redraw each window as accurately as you can on the empty grid below.

You may find this very difficult, in which case you might prefer to study and then recall each window individually - in this case spend up to 30 seconds trying to memorise each window.

> What's in the Windows?

Redraw each window as accurately as you can below:

> The Flip Side of Memory

This is an interesting test of your visual memory because it requires you to both recall and manipulate an image simultaneously.

Firstly study the top image for no more than one minute, then cover it over and try to redraw it on the grid below. But don't just draw it as it was - instead draw it as if reflected in the dashed red line 'mirror'. A few elements are given to help you along the way.

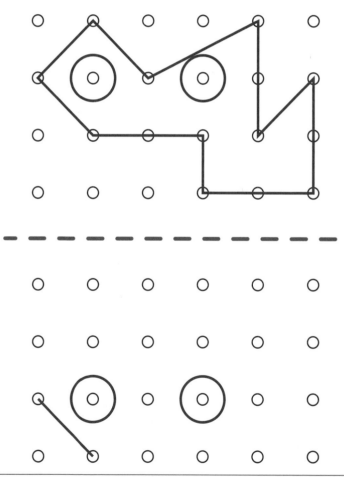

> **Negative Calcudoku**

Can you place 1, 2, 3, -1, -2 and -3 into each row and column while also obeying the boxed region constraints? The number at the top-left of each boxed region gives the result of applying the given operator between all the numbers in that region. So for example the two boxes in a "3+" region should contain 1 and 2. If the operator is subtraction or division then start the calculation with the highest value in the box, so for example a region with a 1, 3 and -3 in any order could be a solution to "5-". You can repeat a number within a region, subject to not repeating any numbers in a row or column.

You'll need to remember how to deal with negative numbers for this one! For example **2 – -1 = 3**, and **-2 × -3 = 6**.

Values to place: **-3 -2 -1 1 2 3**					
2–		6–		0+	1–
3+		1÷			
3–			12×		
3–				4–	
5–		2÷		3×	
			1+		

> Number Anagram

Given the following set of numbers and mathematical signs, can you rearrange them in order to obtain each of the given results?

You must use all of the numbers and signs, but you can use as many additional 'brackets' as you like - for example: (4x5)-(2x3)=14.

2	4	7	9	75
+	+	×	×	

Result: 149

Result: 853

> Writing Back-words

Can you solve each of these pairs of clues? The solution to both clues is the same except that one is written backwards compared to the other. For example, the solution to a pair of clues might be WOLF and FLOW. The number in brackets is the number of letters in the solution.

Domestic animals (4) **Put one leg in front of the other**

Dug for minerals (5) **Hard-wearing cotton fabric**

Show appreciation with a gift (6) **Storage compartment**

Provide as expected (7) **Despised**

Under pressure (8) **Sweet courses**

> Word Pyramid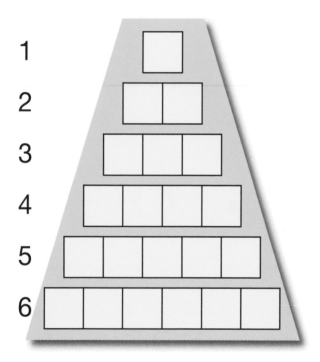

By writing a single letter in each brick can you make each row of bricks spell out a word? Each level of the pyramid uses exactly the same set of bricks as the layer below, but one brick is removed and the order also may change. For example, 'TAR' could be on the row above 'CART'. Each word must also fit the given clue.

1
2
3
4
5
6

> 1: Indefinite article
> 2: Father
> 3: Appropriate
> 4: Knocks lightly
> 5: Italian food
> 6: Adjusts

> Initial Thoughts

If each of the following acronyms actually existed, what do you think they might stand for in the given context?

As an example, **OVS** could be "**O**ver-enthusiastic **V**olunteer **S**yndrome" in the charity industry.

> # F Y F
> ## (Dieting industry)

> # R W W
> ## (Cosmetics industry)

> # S D S
> ## (Football players)

> Spinning Around

Can you copy each grid onto the other while rotating all of the lines in the manner indicated by the arrows? The grid of dots is provided for reference.

In other words, copy the top grid by rotating clockwise 90 degrees onto the bottom grid; and copy the bottom grid onto the top grid by rotating 90 degrees anti-clockwise (counter-clockwise).

If you complete this task successfully then you will reveal a stylised image.

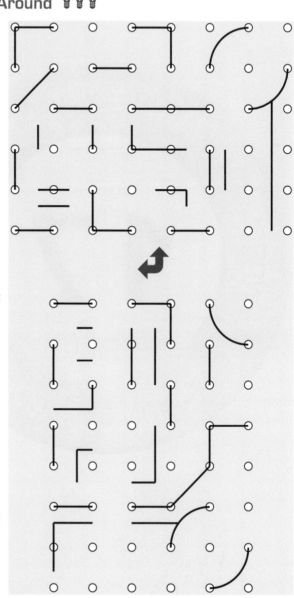

> Light It Up 💡💡

When you mix coloured lights you end up with different colours.

Can you work out what colour will result when merging light of each of the following pairs of colours?

> Inequality Sudoku

> Place 1 to 6 into each row, and column, plus each bold-lined 2x3 box, while obeying the inequality signs.

> Less than ("<") and greater than (">") signs between some squares indicate that the values in these two squares must be greater than or less than one another as indicated by the sign. The sign always points towards the smaller number.

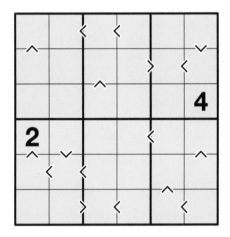

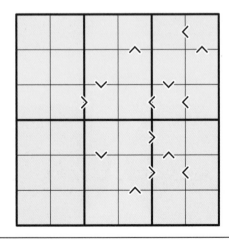

> Set Phrase-rs to Stun 💡💡💡

Can you work out which phrase each of these pictures is hiding?

For example, "GAit'sallME" could be "It's all in the game".

Sun	Sun	Sun	Sun	Sun	Sun	Sun
1	2	3	4	5	6	7
8	9	10	11	12	13	14
15	16	17	18	19	20	21
22	23	24	25	26	27	28
29	30	31				

Never

> Tree-mendous Memory

It's time for another visual memory workout. Learning to quickly study an image or scene and pick out and recall key details is a very useful skill.

Start by covering the opposite page, then study the evening scene below for no more than 30 seconds. Then cover over this page instead and reveal the opposite page, which you will need to rotate around to read, and follow the instructions there.

> **Tree-mendous Recall**

Look at the version of the picture on this page. There are five differences to find. Can you spot them all?

If you get stuck, study this image for 30 seconds and then flip back to the first one to see if you can see the remaining differences. (And so on, until you have spotted them all!)

> Balancing Act

Look at the four balances below and see if you can work out which of the four different objects weighs the **least**.

Also, which of the objects weighs the **most**?

Assume that distance from the fulcrum (the centre of the balance) has no effect on the result.

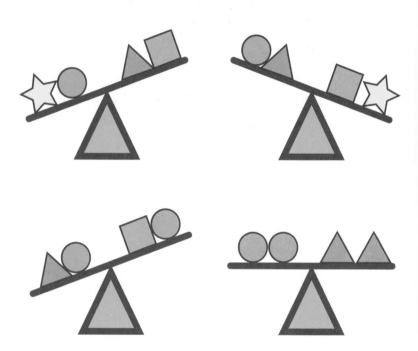

> Brain Chain

How good is your mental arithmetic? See how quickly you can solve each of the following brain chains without making any written notes. Start with the number on the left and follow the arrows while applying each operation in turn. Write the result in the empty box at the end.

| **50** | ×3 | 2/3 of this | +114 | -168 | **RESULT** |

| **20** | Add thirty-five percent | +92 | -3 | ÷2 | **RESULT** |

| **36** | 1/2 of this | +10 | 75% of this | ×5 | **RESULT** |

| **18** | +110 | 25% of this | 3/4 of this | +91 | **RESULT** |

| **116** | 75% of this | Add twenty-two | Multiply by two | -38 | **RESULT** |

> Vowel Play

In each of the following words all of the vowels have been deleted.

Can you work out what each of the original words was?

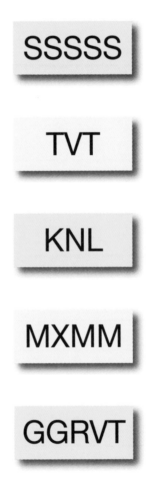

SSSSS

TVT

KNL

MXMM

GGRVT

> Word Pairs

Match each word with one other word so that when joined together they make up a new word. For example, 'DOG' and 'MA' could be joined to form 'DOGMA'.

AIR	LET
BOY	LINE
BRACE	MILL
BUTTER	SET
CAT	TREAD
COW	TUNE
DOWN	TURN
FLY	UP
FOR	WALK

>> CREATIVITY

> Fridge Magnets

Imagine rearranging the fridge magnets below. What interesting sentences and phrases can you come up with? Write them on the freezer cabinet below! You can use each word multiple times.

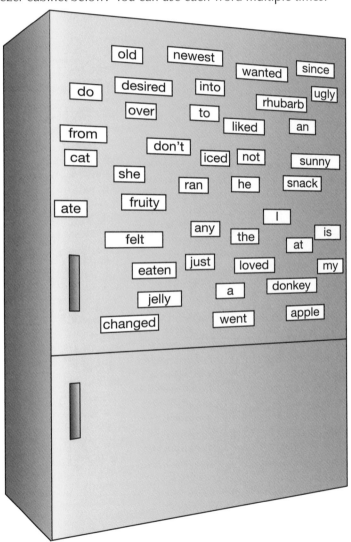

> Pattern Pairings

Each of the following patterns occurs twice, so can you match each pattern with its identical partner? The patterns are rotated with respect to one another, but none of them are reflected or manipulated in any other way.

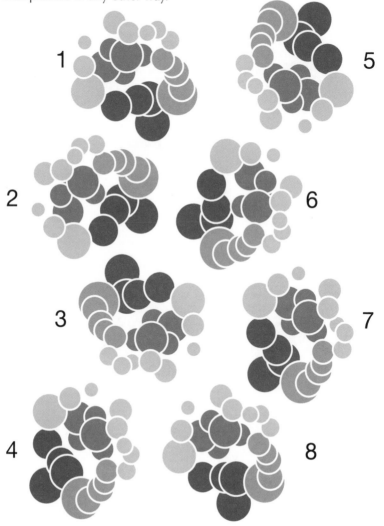

> Single Stroke

Can you draw this pattern in a single stroke without taking your pen off the paper or drawing any line more than once? Crossing over an existing line is allowed.

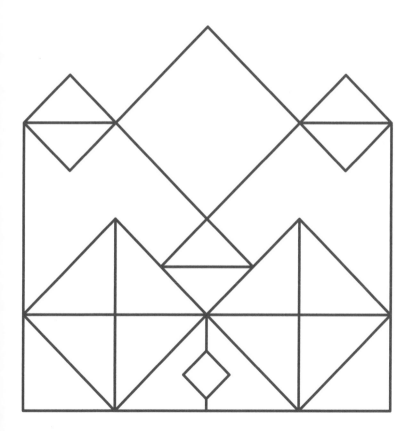

>> REASONING

> Jigsaw Sudoku

You can't make regular Sudoku in a 7x7 version because the 1x7 or 7x1 boxes would simply duplicate the rows or columns. But for Jigsaw Sudoku it adds a surprising amount of extra difficulty, relative to 6x6. Can you fit 1 to 7 into each row, column and bold-lined jigsaw piece?

> Logical Sequence

Can you work out what transformation rules is being used to move from each pattern in the left column to the next one, as shown by the green arrows?

By applying the same transformation rules to the final pattern, which of the labelled options a, b or c should replace the question mark?

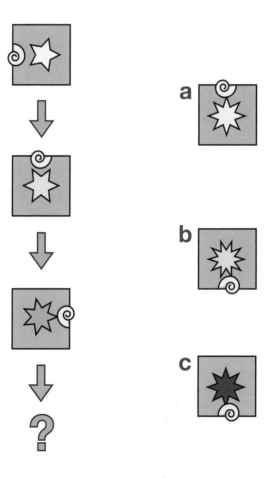

> Fruity Challenge

How good are you at remembering what order some objects are in?

For each row of fruit below, spend 30 seconds trying to remember the order they are in. Next, cover over the fruit, spin the book around and try to number the corresponding fruits on the equivalent set on the opposite page, showing the order they were originally in.

> Set 1

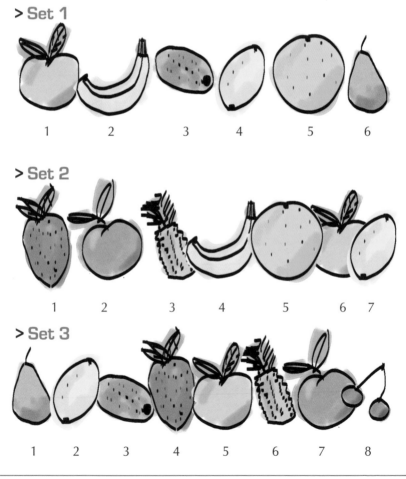

1   2   3   4   5   6

> Set 2

1   2   3   4   5   6   7

> Set 3

1   2   3   4   5   6   7   8

> Order Some Fruit

Please see the opposite page for instructions.

> Set 3

> Set 2

> Set 1

Number each fruit with its original position.

> Order Some Fruit

> **Kakuro**

Place a digit from 1 to 9 into each empty square to solve the clues.
> Each horizontal run of empty squares adds up to the total above
  the diagonal line to the left of the run, and each vertical run of
  empty squares adds up to the total below the diagonal line above
  the run.
> No digit can be used more than once in any run.

> ## Dicey Dilemma

If I roll a single 6-sided die then the likelihood of obtaining a '3' is of course 1 in 6.

See if you can work out these further likelihoods:

> Rolling any double when rolling two dice, such as for example 2 and 2.

> Rolling three dice and having all three show the same value, such as 4 and 4 and 4.

> The likelihood of getting a total of 7 when rolling two dice (for example, 2 and 5).

> If I have just rolled four dice and all four dice show a '6', what is the likelihood that I will get another 6 if I now roll a fifth die?

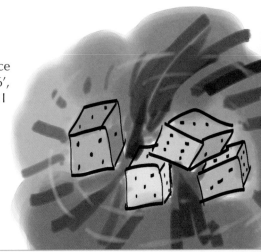

> Letter Trail

How many words of three or more letters can you find by starting on any square in this grid and moving from square to touching square, either right/left/up/down or diagonally, spelling out a word? You cannot use any square more than once in a single word. For example, 'CAP' is okay; 'TAT' is not allowed.

Finding 25 is good; 35 is excellent; 45 is unbelievable!

U	R	E
T	C	R
P	A	E

> puzzLeS

Some puzzles and games are hidden in the grid, placed in one of the following two patterns - either L or S: Can you find them?

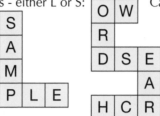

Z	R	Z	G	I	F	L	E	S	L	R
F	S	R	H	R	W	H	A	N	I	Q
E	I	A	A	A	U	Q	P	E	T	V
N	A	I	N	P	A	R	K	Q	U	A
C	E	S	J	I	E	O	A	G	J	L
K	S	D	M	D	N	U	K	Y	T	I
Y	E	R	B	D	H	S	U	R	O	F
S	C	R	L	S	I	E	B	A	F	S
L	T	A	N	U	T	T	R	R	A	G
R	E	P	G	D	O	R	I	A	O	U
L	S	E	L	O	K	U	D	G	E	G

BRIDGE   FENCES   HANJIE   HITORI
INEQUALITY   KAKURO   RECTANGLES   SKYSCRAPER
SUDOKU   WRAPAROUND

> Sliding Around

A good imagination will definitely help you with this puzzle. A pair of scissors and possibly some cardboard and glue/tape are also useful, however!

Start by cutting out the coloured pieces at the bottom of the opposite page. You might want to glue or tape them to a piece of cardboard first to make them more sturdy.

Next, place them on the empty board below in the exact arrangement shown at the top of the opposite page.

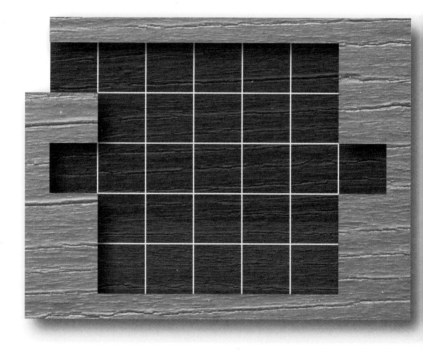

The aim of the task is to work out how to make the red piece, marked with a brown circle, escape from the puzzle board.

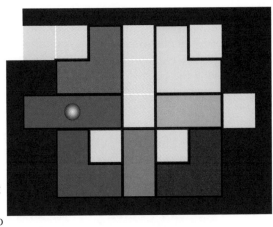

The pieces can be moved up, down, left or right (but not diagonally) from square to square, so that the edges remain aligned with the white grid lines.

No two pieces can ever overlap, even during a move, and you cannot rotate or flip over any piece. They must stay in the orientation shown above. Also no piece can stick outside the puzzle board at any time - the only piece that can leave is the red one, and only once it has reached the exit!

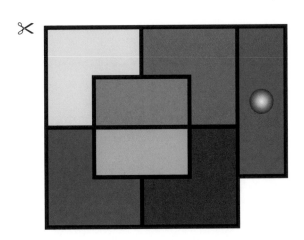

> Sliding Further

Once you've completed (or given up on!) the puzzle on the previous page, try this second one using exactly the same puzzle board and rules, but with the yellow piece placed in a different orientation. This small alternation creates an entirely new (and even harder!) puzzle.

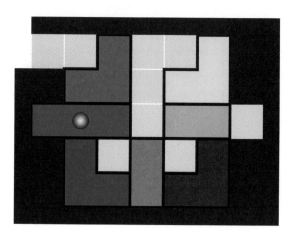

This area will be cut out
(see previous page)

> Combined Approach

Mentally try to combine the two images below, so the white squares on one are replaced with the contents of the coloured squares from the other, and vice-versa.

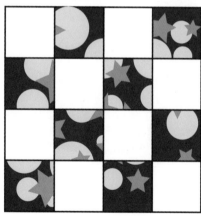

> How many yellow circles are there?
> How many orange stars can you count?
> Can you count how many yellow circles there are which aren't overlapped in any way by a star?

> Cut Out Cubes

All except one of the following shapes can be cut out and folded along the lines to form a six-sided cube.

Which is the odd one out that won't form a complete cube?

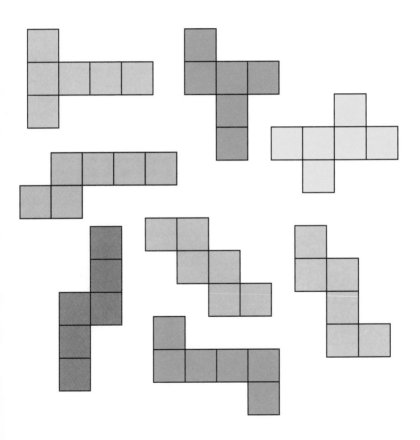

> Solo Battleships

You've probably played the classic two-player pencil and paper game, but did you know that you can also play Battleships in a solo version?

> Locate the listed set of hidden ships of various lengths in the grid.
> Each ship can be placed horizontally or vertically only, and cannot touch another ship horizontally or vertically (diagonally is okay).
> Numbers next to each row or column specify the number of filled ship segments in that row/column.

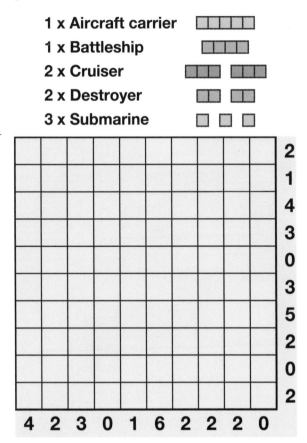

1 x Aircraft carrier

1 x Battleship

2 x Cruiser

2 x Destroyer

3 x Submarine

> Dominoes 💡💡💡

Can you place a full set of dominoes into the grid?

> Draw along the dashed lines to indicate where each domino is placed.
> Use the chart to check off dominoes you've already placed.
> 0 represents a blank on a domino.
> Each domino occurs exactly once in the grid.

5	6	0	6	2	5	1	1
2	4	3	5	1	1	6	6
2	3	6	1	6	0	2	1
0	0	0	0	2	4	2	0
5	1	3	4	4	3	5	4
4	4	2	5	3	2	6	3
0	5	5	1	4	3	3	6

0	1	2	3	4	5	6	
							0
							1
							2
							3
							4
							5
							6

> Vegetable Feast

First of all cover over the opposite page. Next, study the following collection of vegetables for no more than one minute.

When time is up, cover over this page and reveal the opposite one. Can you work out exactly which vegetables have been eaten?

You will need to rotate the book first.

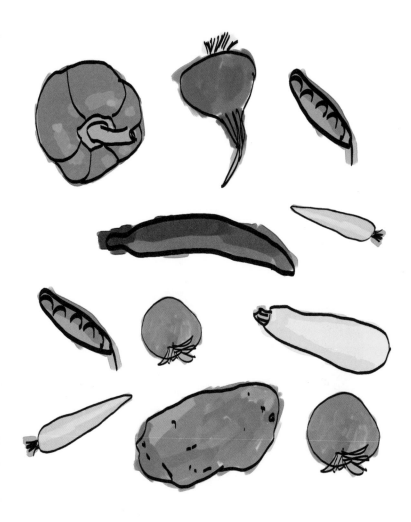

Can you draw the missing vegetables?

Instructions are on the opposite page.

> **Vegetable Feast** (continued)

> Age Awareness

At school one day a teacher is asked by a pupil how old each of her four children is, and this is what she says:

> One year from now, Andrea will be two thirds of Barbara's age

> The combined total of Andrea, Barbara and Christina's ages is 16

> Debbie is three years older than Christina

> Five years from now, Debbie will be twice as old as Andrea.

Can you work out how old each of her four children is?

> Furniture Fun

A new item of storage furniture is being installed into a large warehouse. Considering it as a perfect cuboid, it takes up 3m by 4m of floor space and is 12m tall:

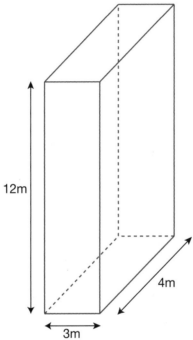

> What is the total length of all twelve edges of this piece of furniture?

> What is the volume of space occupied by this item?

> If the interior is empty, what is the length of the longest perfectly straight rod you can possibly store inside the furniture?

> Flying Letters

By picking in order one letter from the outer orbit, one letter from the middle orbit and then one letter from the inner-most orbit, how many three letter English words can you find? For example, 'ARE'. There are at least 15 more to find.

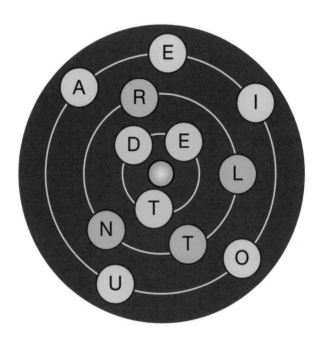

> ## Mixed-up Words 💡💡💡💡💡

In each of the following sentences, find an anagram of the CAPITALISED word that will fit into the gap.

> The STUDENT didn't do much work, so his learning was _____.

> She studied the _____ that outlined the details of her CATECHISM.

> The first EARTH-BORN aliens looked oddly _____.

> Instead of being CREATIVE, the agency ended up being _____.

> There was a TANGIBLE noise; the sound of _____.

> He hid in AMONG the _____ trees.

> She found the STEADIEST boat to take her _____.

> Cubic Construction

The picture below might appear to some to be an isometric wire mesh projection of a 3×4×5 cuboid. But that's not what it really is! No, lying hidden in among these lines is something that's easy to miss.

What might be hidden? Shade in your choice of areas to reveal a creative image of your own. See page 48 for an example.

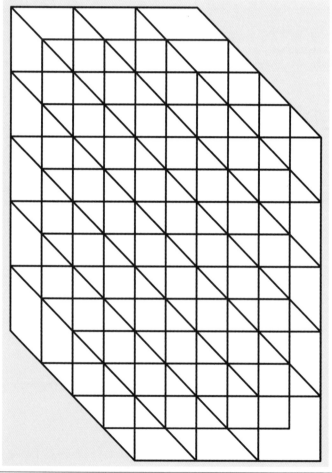

> Cutting Issue

Can you draw exactly three completely straight lines in order to divide this shape into four areas, such that all the areas contain one each of the three different circle sizes and colours?

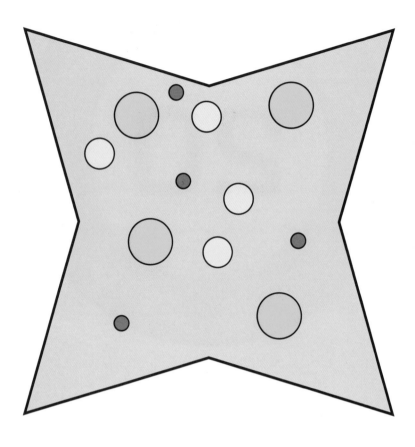

> Circuit Breaker

A piece is missing from this electronic circuit. Can you pick which one of the four pieces below fits into the gap in order to complete the circuit? Once complete all of the lines will connect at both ends. You may need to rotate the correct piece.

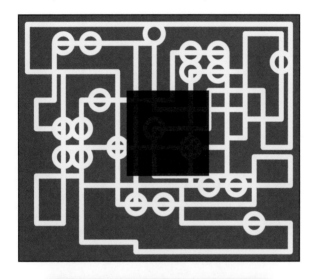

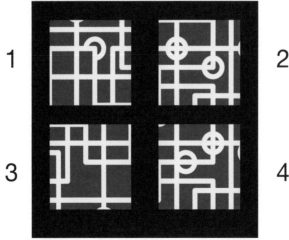

1
2
3
4

> Slitherlink

Draw a single loop by connecting together the dots so that each numbered square has the specified number of adjacent line segments.

> Dots can only be joined by horizontal or vertical lines.
> The loop cannot touch, cross or overlap itself in any way.

3	1	1	2	3	3
2	2		0		2
		3		0		2
3		0			3
3		0		2	3
3	1	2	2	1	1

1		3		3		2	
3		1		1		1	1
3	2				2	2	
2		2	2		3		
		2		2	2		3
	1	0				1	1
3	1		0		3		2
3		3		1		1	

> Hitori 💡💡💡

Shade in squares so that no number occurs
more than once per row or column.

> Shaded squares cannot touch in either a
  horizontal or vertical direction.
> All unshaded squares must form a single
  continuous area

You may find it helpful to circle numbers you
know are definitely *not* shaded.

2	5	6	2	4	6
1	6	5	4	6	3
3	3	1	2	2	5
3	1	4	5	6	2
5	4	2	1	3	1
6	4	6	3	6	5

5	3	7	4	8	2	1	5
1	6	6	8	3	4	2	7
6	4	8	7	1	3	5	3
2	6	6	1	6	5	6	4
6	5	2	4	7	3	8	3
7	6	5	2	4	1	4	8
4	1	8	5	2	3	7	6
5	6	4	3	1	7	1	1

> Visual Detail

It's time to test your visual memory again.

Look at the six different cloud weather pictures below. Just the cloud parts are repeated on the page opposite, but by spending no more than two minutes studying the pictures below can you accurately redraw the rest of each weather pattern? Cover over this page once your memorisation time is up.

> Visual Recall

Instructions are on the opposite page.

Try to redraw each cloud weather picture as accurately as possible. Use of colour is, however, entirely optional!

> Calcudoku

Can you place 1 to 7 into each row and column while also obeying the boxed region constraints? The number at the top-left of each boxed region gives the result of applying the given operator between all the numbers in that region. So for example the two boxes in a "3+" region should contain 1 and 2. If the operator is subtraction or division then start the calculation with the highest value in the box, so for example a region with a 1, 3 and 5 in any order could be a solution to "1-". You can repeat a number within a region, subject to not repeating any numbers in a row or column.

1÷	21×		5×		21+	
		33+	1−			
90×			28×			6×
2−					7×	
	12+	3÷				
		9+			126×	
		6×		30×		

> Number Pyramid

Can you complete the building of this number pyramid?

Each brick should contain a value equal to the sum of the two blocks directly beneath it.

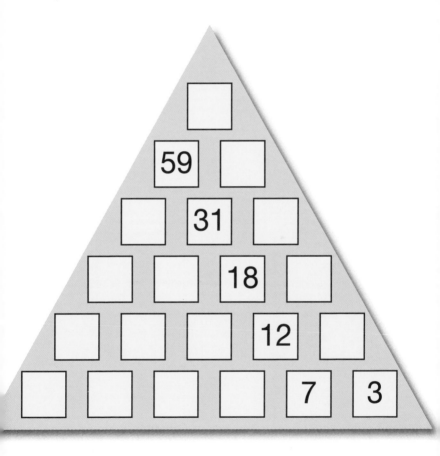

> Word Slider

The picture below shows a 'word slider'. By moving each of the six sliders up and down, you can spell words out through the window in the middle.

Simply by imagining moving the sliders up and down, how many regular English words of six letters can you spell out? One word is spelled out for you already.

There are around 14 reasonably well-known words, so getting to 10 words is pretty good; getting more than 14 is fantastic.

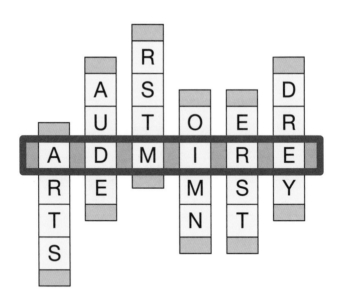

> Missing Pairs

For each line can you find the pair of letters that will fit into all of the gaps to make English words?

For example, 'LT' will fit into FA__ER, FI__HY and PA__RY to make FALTER, FILTHY and PALTRY.

| HA__ER | MA__AL | SU__ER |

| AF__AT | ME__DY | UN__AD |

| PA__ON | OU__UN | CI__US |

| WH__SH | GL__MY | CH__SE |

| ST__ED | SK__ER | LE__AY |

| BU__ER | PO__OM | TE__LE |

>> CREATIVITY

> Objective Obfuscation

You've probably made a cup of tea using a tea bag, but rip open that bag and tip it out and you can make yourself a handy mouth protector to stop flies getting in your mouth while you go for a run. Very useful.

What unusual uses for the following objects can you come up? They can be as ridiculous as you like!

> Two pens and an elastic band

> A glass vase

> A mile of washing line cord

> A packet of sticky notes

> A stack of brain-training books

> Private Roads

Can you connect each pair of identical numbers together using only horizontal and vertical lines from square to square? Only one line can enter any square, so in other words the lines can't touch or cross.

Take a look at the example solution on the right to be sure you understand the rules.

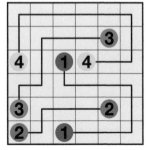

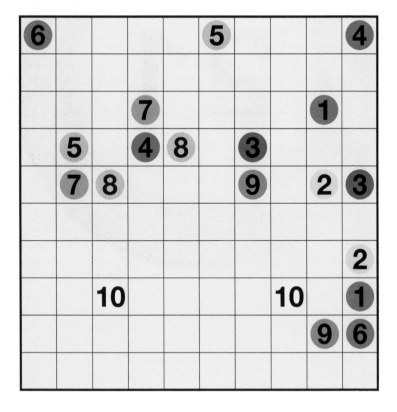

> Over and Over and Over

The first three illustrations on this page each contains two words, one overlaid on top of the other. Can you work out what the two words are in each case? For the final illustration there are three overlaid words - can you also work out what all three of these words are?

problem

overlay

gemsine

threes

> Skyscraper

Place each number from 1 to 6 into every row and column.

> Each number in the completed grid represents a building of that many storeys. Place the buildings in such a way that each given number outside the grid represents the number of buildings that can be seen from that point, looking only at that number's row or column.

> A building with a higher value always obscures a building with a lower value, while a building with a lower value never obscures a building with a higher value.

	1	3	2	2	4	2	
1							3
3							2
2							3
5							2
4							1
2							2
	4	1	3	3	3	2	

> Hanjie

Shade in squares in the grid to reveal a picture while obeying the clue constraints at the start of each row or column.

- > The clues provide, in order from the left or the top, a list of the length of every run of consecutive shaded squares in each row or column.
- > Multiple runs in a row/column are separated by at least one empty square. For example "2,3" means there is a run of 2 shaded squares, followed by at least one empty square, and then 3 consecutive shaded squares.
- > Take a look at the example above to see how the clues correspond with the solution.

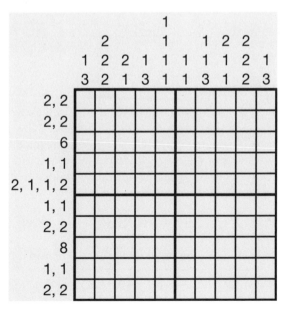

Clue: Time to hide?

> Memory Search

This Memory Search is similar to those that have come before, but this one is in two halves.

First, spend no more than one minute memorising the list immediately below of twelve sporting events. Next, cover over this entire page and see if you can find them all in the word search on the opposite page - words run in a straight line either horizontally, vertically or diagonally, and may read backwards as well as forwards. No peeking back at the word list, but when you're finished (or stuck) then read the instructions in 'Step Two' opposite.

BOWLING	CRICKET	POLO
FENCING	CROQUET	SKIING
BADMINTON	JUDO	TENNIS
DRESSAGE	GOLF	ROWING

> Feeling Sportier

Have a look at the words you previously memorised above. Are there any you failed to recall? If so, highlight these. Now spend no more than one minute memorising any words highlighted above plus the additional ten sporting events listed below. Once your minute is up, cover over both word lists again and try to find the remaining words in the word search opposite.

MARATHON	LACROSSE	ANGLING
VOLLEYBALL	KARATE	ARCHERY
ORIENTEERING	HANDBALL	GYMNASTICS
	SKYDIVING	

> Search and Recall

Instructions are on the opposite page. How many of the sporting events can you recall?

R	R	L	D	E	H	R	K	A	R	A	T	E
I	G	G	L	R	S	A	O	P	V	D	G	C
S	H	N	N	A	E	S	N	W	O	N	V	I
A	N	I	I	I	B	S	O	D	I	L	I	S
A	T	L	C	C	V	Y	S	R	B	N	O	G
G	E	G	R	O	N	I	E	A	C	A	G	N
N	U	N	I	G	R	E	D	L	G	A	L	I
I	Q	A	C	V	T	M	F	Y	L	E	L	L
I	O	T	K	N	I	E	T	L	K	O	W	W
K	R	T	E	N	N	I	S	T	O	S	V	O
S	C	I	T	S	A	N	M	Y	G	G	D	B
O	R	O	Y	R	E	H	C	R	A	U	R	O
O	N	O	H	T	A	R	A	M	J	C	A	O

> Step Two

Once you are finished (or stuck), uncover the opposite page and read the instructions in the bottom section under 'Feeling Sportier'.

> Number Anagram

Given the following set of numbers and mathematical signs, can you rearrange them in order to obtain each of the given results?

You must use all of the numbers and signs, but you can use as many additional 'brackets' as you like - for example: (4x5)-(2x3)=14.

3	4	6	7	50
+	+	×	÷	

Result: 552

Result: 234

> Multiplic-alien

Your friendly neighbourhood alien, Zox, has landed on planet Z2 and sets about constructing a prosperous colony. As part of this he has to populate the planet with his Zalien offspring.

Zox and the lovely Zoxina have six children of their own, and then in time each of their children take partners from elsewhere in the colony and have five children of their own each too. Then each of these children take partners from outside the family and have four children of their own. Each of these great grandchildren is given a pet zog at birth.

Now it's time to test your multiplic-alien skills:

> How many zogs are there in total among all of Zox's great grandchildren?

> How many people are there in Zox's family, counting him and Zoxina plus all of his descendants and their partners? Don't include the pet zogs.

> If each generation had produced twice as many children per couple, how many zogs would there have now been?

> Fishy Trail

Can you draw a path that visits every letter in the grid, spelling out a series of fish? The last letter of each fish is also the first letter of the following fish, and you may only move left, right, up or down between letters. Every single letter must be used once and once only in the final path. The start and end of the path are given. Some fish are made up of multiple words (for example 'strawberry grouper' would be two words but a single fish).

A	N	L	L	O	C	K	O	K	A
H	C	E	O	D	D	I	R	E	N
O	V	Y	W	H	A	N	R	E	E
K	C	A	J	C	R	G	E	H	L
I	N	G	F	N	O	U	P	S	I
A	H	S	I	E	T	U	E	I	O
L	I	B	U	T	O	O	R	F	N
M	A	H	S	I	A	R	A	I	N
M	A	D	A	F	D	T	W	O	B
E	E	R	B	O	U	B	R	D	E
R	H	E	A	M	T	H	O	O	R

> Odd One Out

In each of the following sets can you work out which of the five words is the odd one out? Most of these are a test of your general knowledge.

> Venus   Jupiter   Pluto
> Earth   Mars

> Athena   Apollo   Hermes
> Zeus   Pluto

> Magnolia   Forsythia   Azalea
> Fuchsia   Buddleia

> Triangle   Entangle   Alerting
> Integral   Relating

> Initial Thoughts

If each of the following acronyms actually existed, what do you think they might stand for in the given context?

As an example, **OVS** could be "**O**ver-enthusiastic **V**olunteer **S**yndrome" in the charity industry.

N S L Y
(Publishing industry)

P D T B
(Postal workers)

S E T P
(Fast food restaurants)

> Layer by Layer

What is the minimum selection of patterns, 1 to 8, which you can overlay in order to form the composite image at the bottom? If there is more than one way of making the pattern then you must find the minimal set (the smallest number of patterns required).

You may not rotate or reflect the patterns, and there must be no 'extra' lines in the result compared to the target image.

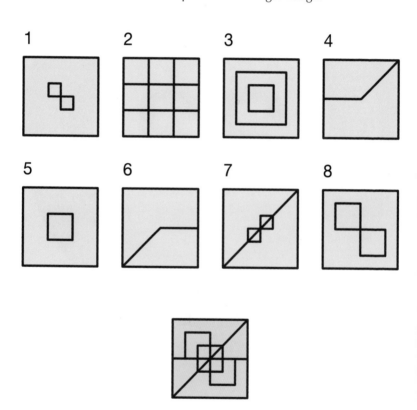

> Turn it Around 💡💡💡

For each of the three patterns in the top row, which of the three options below would result if you were to rotate that pattern as indicated by each arrow? (So 90 degrees clockwise, 180 degrees and 90 degrees anti-clockwise/counter-clockwise respectively)

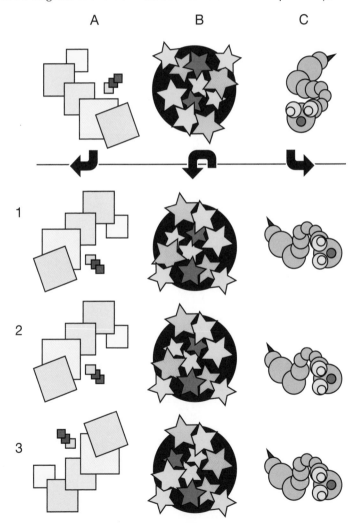

> Sudoku

Since it was first published in Western newspapers in late 2004, Sudoku has become almost ubiquitous. But in case you don't yet know the rules: Can you place 1 to 9 into every row, column and bold-lined 3x3 box?

4			1	6	2			9
		5				7		
	6						1	
2			4		5			1
5								7
7			6		1			8
	4						2	
		9				8		
6			8	3	9			5

> Light-Up

Place light bulbs in empty squares so that all of the empty squares in the puzzle either contain a bulb or are at lit up by at least one bulb.

> Light bulbs illuminate all squares in the same row and column up to the first black square encountered in each direction.
> No light bulb may illuminate any other light bulb, although empty squares may be lit by more than one bulb.
> Some black squares contain numbers - these numbers indicate how many light bulbs are placed in the neighbouring squares immediately adjacent above, below, to the right and left of these black squares.
> Not all light bulbs are necessarily clued via black squares.

> Remember the Difference

Cover over the bottom half of this page and then study the country scene on the right for no more than 30 seconds. Then cover over the top half of the page instead and rotate the book

around to follow the upside-down instructions below.

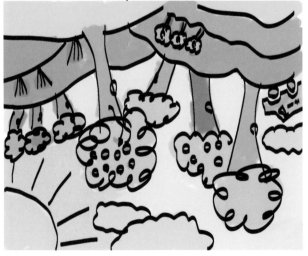

them there.

can spot

you

see if

to

original

the

back to

then flipping

instead and

this image

memorising

try

can't,

you

If

them all?

Can you spot

> Recall the Difference

There are **six** differences between this image and the one you have just remembered.

> It's On The Cards 💡💡💡💡

First of all cover over the bottom half of this page. Next, spend up to one minute trying to memorise the top arrangement of ten cards. Once time is up, cover over the top half while revealing the bottom half, and try to recall which card was in which place. You will be given either the number or the suit - and sometimes a clue to the number as well - in each case.

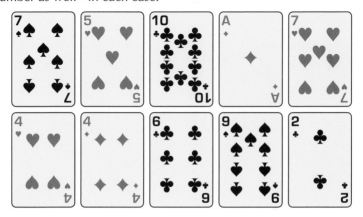

> Reveal Your Cards

Can you recall each card? Green colour is used for the lone numbers in order to not reveal whether the suit is red or black.

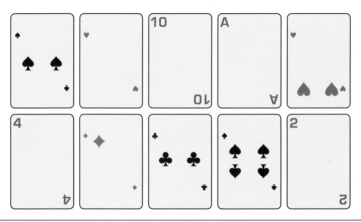

> Kakuro

Place a digit from 1 to 9 into each empty square to solve the clues.

> Each horizontal run of empty squares adds up to the total above the diagonal line to the left of the run, and each vertical run of empty squares adds up to the total below the diagonal line above the run.

> No digit can be used more than once in any run.

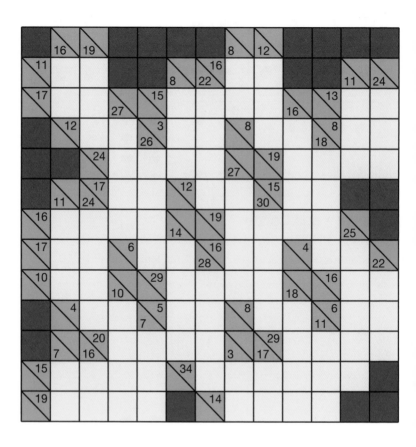

> **Number Darts**

By choosing exactly one number from each ring of this dartboard, can you find three segments whose values add up to each of the listed totals?

For example, to reach a total of 119 you would take 28 from the outer ring, 48 from the middle ring and 43 from the inner ring.

89

99

109

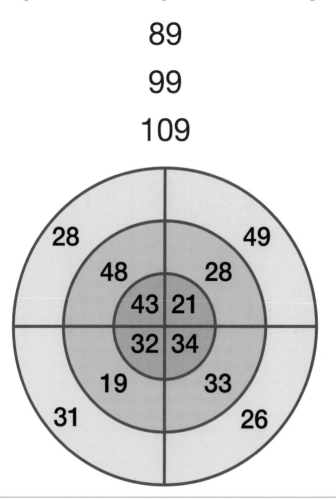

> Letter Trail

How many words of three or more letters can you find by starting on any square in this grid and moving from square to touching square, either right/left/up/down or diagonally, spelling out a word? You cannot use any square more than once in a single word.

Finding 8 is good; 12 is excellent; 14 is amazing!

Z	R	M
I	C	U
O	N	I

> **Word Equations**

In each equation solve the two 'addition' clues to find two separate words that when joined together form a new word that fits the third clue. For example:

Puzzle: Beneath + arise from sitting = comprehend
Solution: UNDER + STAND = UNDERSTAND

1) Officers' quarters + very long periods = communications

2) Not the pros + dine at this? = law enforcement officer

3) Stingy person + having the ability = unhappy

4) Backwards rep? + male descendent = you or me

5) Drinking vessel + piece of wood? = furniture

This pattern is not part of the word equation workout but is the reverse of the creative challenge on the following page!

> Some Reassembly Required

Start by cutting out the square pattern at the bottom of the page, and then cutting along the black lines. You should end up with 8 pieces. Next try to work out how to make each of the following shapes with them. You can rotate or turn over pieces, but not overlap them. Then try to come up with some of your own too!

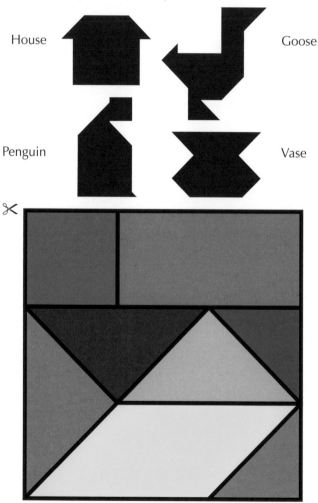

House

Goose

Penguin

Vase

> Comb Over

Can you work out which two of the following halves will join back together to form a complete rounded square? (Like a drinks mat, if you prefer). You won't need to flip any of them over in order to do this.

> Riot of Rectangles 💡💡💡💡💡

This image is packed full of rectangles.

By drawing over existing lines, can you find **18 different squares**?

And once you've done that, can you find an additional **45 non-square rectangles**?

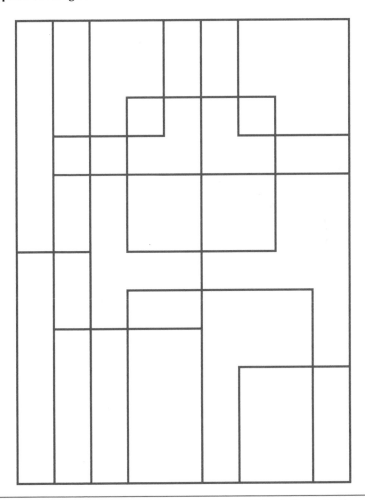

> Wraparound Sudoku

Place 1 to 6 into each row, column and bold-lined jigsaw region.

> Some regions 'wrap around' the outside of the puzzle, travelling off one end of a row/column and continuing on the square at the opposite end of the same row/column.

> Set Phrase-rs to Stun

Can you work out which phrase each of these pictures is hiding? Both of these are a little tricky.

As an example, "GAit'sallME" could be "It's all in the game".

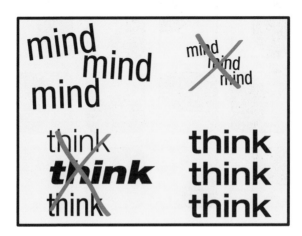

> Grid Memory

Spend up to a minute studying the pattern of shapes in the top grid. Once time is up, cover over the top grid and try to redraw each window as accurately as you can on the empty grid below. Repeating the colours is optional.

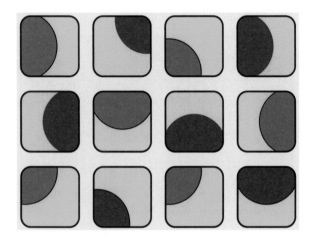

> Down to the Nitty Griddy

Redraw each window as accurately as you can below:

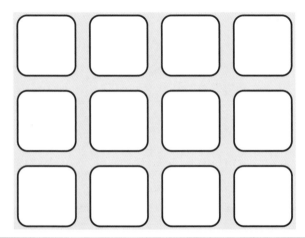

> Memory Recipe

The following list of items are required for a recipe. Each ingredient has a name, a quantity and instructions for its use. Can you remember the entire list?

Cover over the bottom half of the page, then spend up to one minute studying the recipe below. When time is up cover over the top half and reveal the bottom half - can you complete the missing parts?

Quantity	Ingredient	Instruction
500ml	Milk	Pour into bowl
750g	Brown flour	Sieve in
200g	Butter	Add to mix
2	Eggs	Add yolk only
1	Lemon	Grate skin for zest
175g	Brown sugar	Mix in
200g	Currants	Sprinkle on

> Bring Home the Baking

In the following version of the instructions some of the elements are missing. Can you write them all in?

Quantity	Ingredient	Instruction
_____	Milk	_____
750g	Brown flour	_____
200g	_____	Add to mix
_____	Eggs	_____
1	_____	_____
_____	Brown sugar	_____
_____	_____	Sprinkle on

> Brain Chain 💡💡💡💡

How good is your mental arithmetic? See how quickly you can
solve each of the following brain chains without making any written
notes. Start with the number on the left and follow the arrows while
applying each operation in turn. Write the result in the empty box at
the end.

| 174 | 50% of this | Subtract six | 1/3 of this | +477 | RESULT |

| 345 | Two thirds of this | -204 | ×11 | -103 | RESULT |

| 91 | +282 | -190 | 1/3 of this | +184 | RESULT |

| 421 | Add three hundred and one | -252 | 4/5 of this | -50% | RESULT |

| 185 | ÷5 | Multiply by eight | 1/2 of this | +20 | RESULT |

> Killer Sudoku

Killer Sudoku is regular Sudoku with an added killer twist!

Not only do you need to place 1 to 9 into each row, column and 3x3 bold-lined box, but you must also place numbers so that they add up to the total given at the top-left of each dashed-line cage. You also can **not** repeat a number within a dashed-line cage (this restriction actually makes the puzzle easier, not harder, because it eliminates some possibilities).

> Swapping Around

Copy each column of letters and blanks from the top grid into the identical column in the empty grid below. As you do so rearrange the letters and blanks in each column so that reading left to right and top to bottom the grid spells out a quote by a famous historical figure, followed by their name. A single shaded square is placed between **all** words, representing a space.

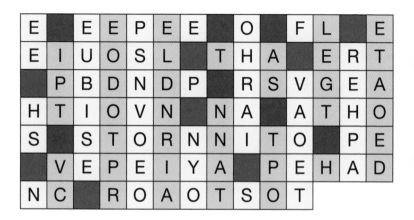

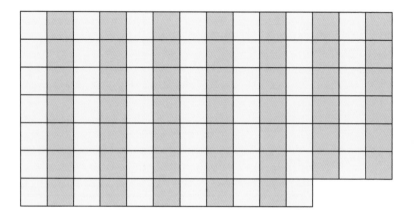

> Word Pyramid

By writing a single letter in each brick can you make each row of bricks spell out a word? Each level of the pyramid uses exactly the same set of bricks as the layer below, but one brick is removed and the order also may change. For example, 'TAR' could be on the row above 'CART'. Each word must also fit the given clue.

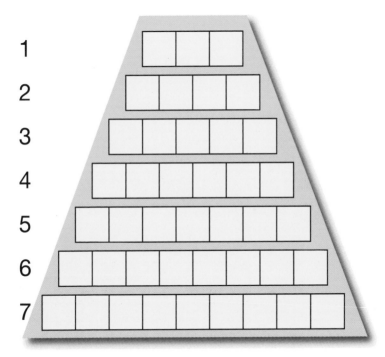

> 1: Consumed
> 2: Group of collaborators
> 3: Domesticates
> 4: Perfect something
> 5: River boat?
> 6: African mongooses
> 7: People who want to sell you something

> Sliding Around

Start by cutting out the coloured pieces at the bottom of the opposite page. You might want to glue or tape them to a piece of cardboard first to make them more sturdy. Next, place them on the empty board below in the exact arrangement shown at the top of the opposite page. You'll have two pieces left over but they're used in the puzzle on the following page.

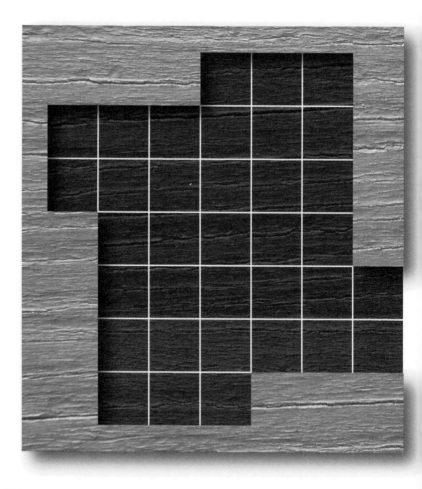

The aim of the task is to work out how to make the red piece, marked with a brown circle, escape from the puzzle board.

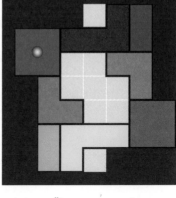

The pieces can be moved up, down, left or right (but not diagonally) from square to square, so that the edges remain aligned with the white grid lines.

No two pieces can ever overlap, even during a move, and you cannot rotate or flip over any piece. They must stay in the orientation shown above. Also no piece can stick outside the puzzle board at any time - the only piece that can leave is the red one, and only once it has reached the exit!

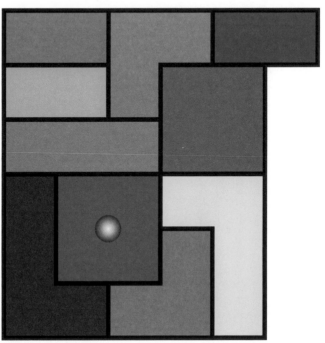

> Sliding Further

Once you've completed (or given up on!) the puzzle on the previous page, try this second one using exactly the same puzzle board and rules, but with a different selection from the pieces you previously cut out.

This second puzzle, while still hard, is actually considerably easier than the one on the previous page!

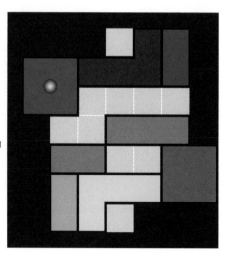

This area will be cut out
(see previous page)

> **Four Piece Arrangement**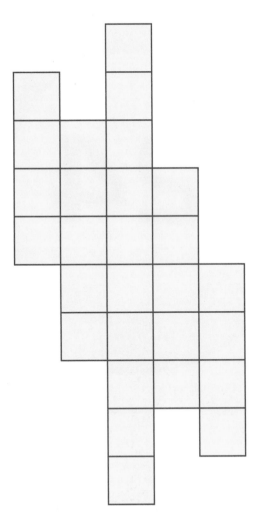

By drawing along the existing lines, can you divide this shape up into four identical pieces, with no pieces left over? The pieces may be rotated versions of one another but you cannot flip or 'turn over' any of the pieces.

> Circuit Breaker

A piece is missing from this electronic circuit. Can you pick which one of the four pieces below fits into the gap in order to complete the circuit? Once complete all of the lines will connect at both ends. You may need to rotate the correct piece.

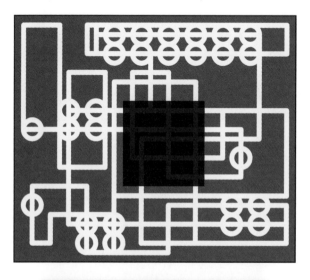

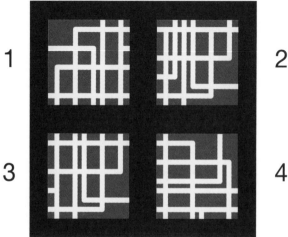

1

2

3

4

> Card Box

Can you place each of the nine following cards into the 3x3 grid, with one card per box?

Place the cards so that:

> Every row and column increases or decreases in number value as you read left-to-right or top-to-bottom.
> A ♣ and a ♦ are both in the same row.
> The centre square, B2, contains the **6♣**.
> Both column A and row 1 have two ♥s.
> Square B1 is less than square A1 in number value
> The numbers in column B add up to 17.

	A	B	C
1			
2			
3			

> PivotPix

Draw along the dashed grid lines so that each pivot circle ends up at the centre of exactly one shape, and so that every square in the grid is used by exactly one shape. All shapes must have pivots.

> Each shape must be symmetrical in such a way that if rotated through 180 degrees around the pivot it would look exactly the same.

> Once the puzzle is complete, shade in each shape with the colour of their pivot circle to reveal a hidden picture.

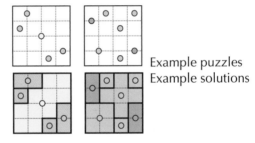

Example puzzles
Example solutions

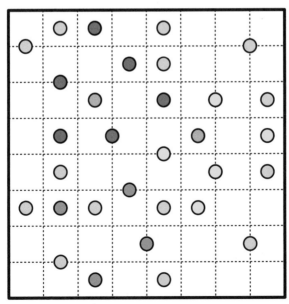

> Out of Shape

First of all cover over the bottom half of the page. Next, study the geometric shapes immediately below for no more than one minute. When time is up, cover over the top half of the page and reveal the bottom of the page. Can you work out exactly which shapes have been removed?

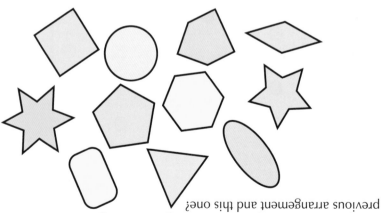

> Shape Down

Can you draw the shapes which have gone missing between the previous arrangement and this one?

> Turned Around

This test of your visual memory requires you to both recall and manipulate an image simultaneously, so you may find it quite tricky!

Firstly study the top image for no more than one minute, then cover it over and try to redraw it on the grid below. But there's a twist - literally. When you redraw it you must rotate the entire image through 180 degrees, as shown by the arrow. A few elements are given to you to help you along the way. Don't just rotate the book!

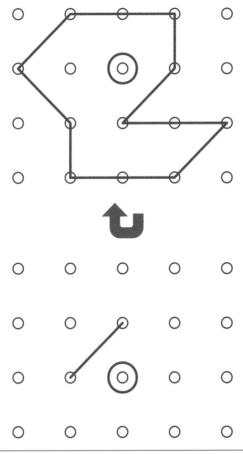

> Calcudoku

Can you place 1 to 8 into each row and column while also obeying the boxed region constraints? The number at the top-left of each boxed region gives the result of applying the given operator between all the numbers in that region. So for example the two boxes in a "3+" region should add to 3, so will contain 1 and 2. If the operator is subtraction or division then start the calculation with the highest value in the box, so for example a region with a 1, 3 and 5 in any order could be a solution to "1-". You can repeat a number within a region, subject to not repeating any numbers in a row or column.

11+	80×		12+	11+		10+	
	6−				2−		10+
12+		6+	24×	32×			
				16×		7+	
10+		4−		5÷	9+	48×	
10×		2−				1−	
	1−		1−	4−	15+		7÷
48×							

> Amazing Journey 🔦🔦🔦

Enter this number maze at the top-left and travel from square to square until you reach the exit, adding up all the numbers you encounter en route from start to finish.

Without entering any square more than once during your journey, can you find a path which adds up to a total of **173**?

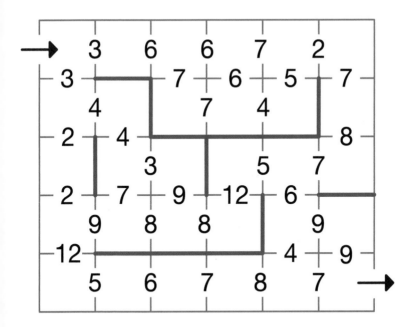

> Word Spinner 🔦🔦🔦🔦🔦

By using the centre letter once plus any other selection of letters (also once each only) from the word spinner below, how many regular English words of three or more letters can you find?

Finding 40 is good; 60 is excellent; 70 is unbelievable!

M O S
C P E
T O I

> Intertwined

Two words of the same length have got mixed up together on each of the following lines, but the letters have remained in the same order. Can you disentangle them and work out what the two original words were? In each case the words are also related to one another in some way.

For example, DCOGAT contains the words 'DOG' and 'CAT'.

MOHUDMEBSLET

EGEXNIPEURST

PCROLTEASMOUTR

DIPROSBPLUTEME

> In-Creasing Creativity

For most of us it's been a while since we folded up paper and cut it with scissors to make patterns, but that's just what this therapeutic and relaxing creative workout is all about!

You'll need some squares of paper for this task. If you don't have any squares handy (those little notelet stacks you can buy are a good source of square paper) then it's easy enough to cut some rectangular paper to size, and you'll need the scissors anyway!

So here's the task: simply by folding a single square of paper one or more times, and then making just one scissors cut in a single straight line, can you make all of the following patterns of holes in a piece of paper?

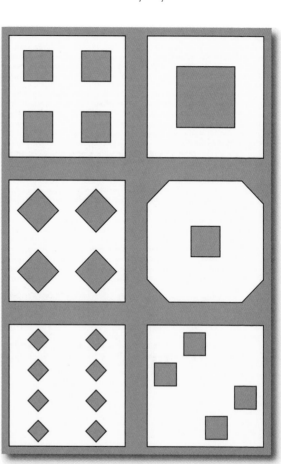

For example for the top-left one you'll need to fold it in half twice and then twice more along the diagonals, then cut off the resulting point.

Feel free to create your own designs too!

Solutions for left-hand pages
appear on the left

Solutions for right-hand pages
appear on the right

> Visualisation

Shape net 'c' is different – the ellipse is turned around compared to the other cubes.

There are 2 blue squares.
There are a total of 8 red, yellow and green squares.

> Reasoning

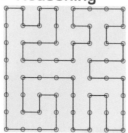

2	2			4		
		9		3	4	
2					2	
	2			8		
10						6
	2			4		
				4		

> Memory

Differences: left ship colour; moon to sun; yellow sand by stream edge; extra hillocks on right; reflections on sea.

> Numbers

The square is lightest.

> There are 13 clubs left out of 49 cards so the likelihood is 13/49.
> Twenty-four red cards remain, so 24/49.
> There's only one 10 of spades, so 1/49.
There are 48 cards remaining of which 11 are hearts, so 11/48.

> Words

Kitten, Calf, Fawn, Lamb, Duckling

At **times**, one of the **items** (or **mites**) **emits** a strange noise.
She is too **scared** to visit the grove of **sacred cedars**.
Travelling through river **deltas**, he hoped his water supply **lasted** as long as **slated**, and regretted eating so much **salted** food.
He washed his **skin** in the **sink** to remove the **inks**.

> Visualisation

Yes, you can draw it in one stroke.

> Reasoning

2	4	1	3
3	1	2	4
4	2	3	1
1	3	4	2

2	3	4	1
4	2	1	3
3	1	2	4
1	4	3	2

1	4	2	3
2	3	4	1
3	2	1	4
4	1	3	2

3	2	4	1
2	3	1	4
4	1	3	2
1	4	2	3

4	3	2	1
3	2	1	4
2	1	4	3
1	4	3	2

> Memory

> Numbers

		17	3	16	4	
	21/14	8	1	9	3	
30	8	3	9	2	7	1
17	9	8	16	4	24	
28	7	1	9	3	8	9
	27	2	7	1	9	8
			8	7	1	

40 - add 1 extra at each step (5, 6, 7 etc)
13 - prime numbers in increasing value
5 - subtract 1 more at each step (-2, -3, -4 etc)
32 - multiply the previous number by 2
1 - divide the previous number by 3

> Words

DREAM, RE**D**ACT, CLAM**P**, PROUD,
POSTED, B**O**ARD, F**L**AVOUR, TABLE**T**,
PAUPER, CHAIR, **B**EAGLE, PEAR**L**

DOUGHNUT, TOFFEE APPLE,
ECLAIRS, SORBET, TIRAMISU,
UPSIDE DOWN PUDDING, GATEAU,
UGLI FRUIT, TAPIOCA, ANGEL CAKES

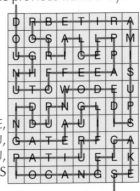

> Visualisation

1B, 2C, 3B

> Reasoning

5	1	3	2	4	6
6	2	5	4	3	1
4	3	6	1	2	5
1	5	2	3	6	4
2	6	4	5	1	3
3	4	1	6	5	2

1	2	5	3	4	6
5	6	1	4	3	2
3	4	2	6	1	5
6	3	4	5	2	1
4	1	6	2	5	3
2	5	3	1	6	4

Person	Trip length	Activity
Harry	5 days	Cycling
Ian	3 days	Golfing
Janet	2 days	Surfing
Karen	7 days	Sunbathing

> Numbers

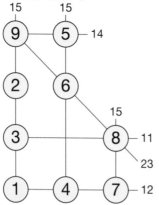

The brain chain results are:

22
100
35
40
26

> Words

1) I V X L C **D** - Roman numbers in increasing order of value

2) J F M A M **J** - months in order: January, February, March, April, May, June

3) N U S J M **E** - planets in our solar system in order from the outermost to the innermost: Neptune, Uranus, Saturn, Jupiter, Mars, Earth

4) F S T F F **S** - ordinal numbers in order: first, second, third, fourth, fifth, sixth

5) O Y G B I **V** - colours in a rainbow, starting at orange: orange, yellow, green, blue, indigo, violet

6) O T T F F **S** - the numbers in order: one, two, three, four, five, six

Possible solutions to the word chains are:

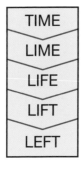
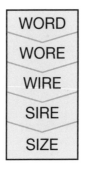
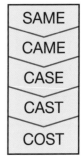

TIME — LIME — LIFE — LIFT — LEFT

WORD — WORE — WIRE — SIRE — SIZE

SAME — CAME — CASE — CAST — COST

>> Week Four

> Visualisation

The top image has 15 cubes on the bottom row, 12 on the middle row and 8 on the top row for a total of 35 cubes.

The lower image has 19 cubes on the bottom row, 12 on the middle row and 8 on the top row for a total of 39 cubes.

It is a letter R.

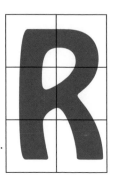

> Reasoning

> Memory

The new wallpaper patterns are:

> Numbers

8x 2	4	8+ 3	1− 1	5
60x 4	40x 1	5	3	1− 2
3	2	1	5	4
5	9+ 3	2÷ 2	4	1
1	5	4	6x 2	3

```
            48
         28    20
      16    12    8
    8    8    4    4
  3    5    3    1    3
```

> Words

Words include: AEGIS, AGE, AGES, AGO, AGONIES, AGONISE, AIR, AIRS, ANGER, ANGERS, ANGRIER, ANISE, ARE, ARES, ARGON, ARISE, ARISEN, AROSE, ARSON, EAR, EARN, EARNS, EARRING, EARRINGS, EARS, EASING, ERA, ERAS, ERASING, GAIN, GAINER, GAINERS, GAINS, GARNER, GARNERS, GARRISON, GAS, GEAR, GEARS, GRAIN, GRAINS, GROAN, GROANS, NAG, NAGS, NEAR, NEARS, OAR, OARING, OARS, ORANGE, ORANGES, ORGAN, ORGANISE, ORGANISER, ORGANS, RAG, RAGE, RAGES, RAGS, RAIN, RAINS, RAISE, RAISER, RAN, RANG, RANGE, RANGER, RANGERS, RANGES, RANGIER, RARE, RARES, RARING, REAR, REARING, REARS, REASON, REGAIN, REGAINS, ROAN, ROANS, ROAR, ROARING, ROARS, SAG, SAGE, SAGER, SAGO, SAN, SANE, SANER, SANG, SARI, SARNIE, SARONG, SEA, SEAR, SEARING, SIERRA, SNAG, SNARE, SOAR, SOARING, SONAR

The hidden words are: DEEDS   ONESELF   GAFFES   ARTIER

> Visualisation

There really are 24 triangles to be found!

> Reasoning

31	32	34	35	43	44	48	49	50
30	33	36	42	45	47	54	53	51
27	29	37	41	46	60	59	55	52
26	28	38	40	61	62	66	58	56
3	25	24	39	63	65	67	71	57
4	2	1	23	64	68	70	73	72
5	11	13	14	22	69	76	75	74
6	10	12	15	18	21	77	78	81
7	8	9	16	17	19	20	80	79

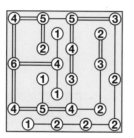

> Memory

H							
A		G		G	I	R	L
M	O	U	S	E			
S		I		R			P
T		N		B			E
E	Y	E	S	I	G	H	T
R		A		L		O	
		P				R	
		I	M	P	I	S	H
D	O	G				E	

> Numbers

3	×	6	÷	9	=	2
×		–		+		
2	×	4	×	8	=	64
–		×		+		
1	×	5	+	7	=	12
=		=		=		
5		10		24		

> The rounded spend is 39
> I spent 38.69, so the difference is 0.31
> Change from a 50.00 note is 11.31
> You can buy the full set of items 25 times

> Words

SHAMPOO
SOOTIEST
TOLERATE
TIPTOP
EQUATIONS (or QUIETENS)

All of the following words can be made:
AIM, AIT, ARM, ART, RAM, RAT, RAY, RIM, SAT, SAY, SIM, SIT, STY,
TAM, TAT, TIT, TRY, WAT, WAY, WIT, WRY

> Visualisation

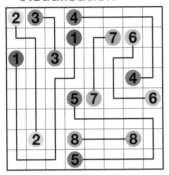

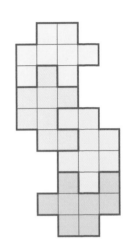

> Reasoning

5	2	4	1	3
1	3	5	4	2
4	1	2	3	5
2	4	3	5	1
3	5	1	2	4

1	3	5	4	2
5	2	4	3	1
3	4	2	1	5
4	5	1	2	3
2	1	3	5	4

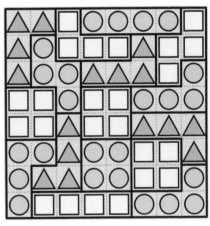

> Memory

Your order should read: 5 6 3 4 1 7 10 8 2 9

> Numbers

$$70 = 28 + 33 + 9$$
$$9 = 19 + 29 + 31$$
$$97 = 28 + 38 + 31$$

> Words

S	A	U	T	T	N	E	I	V	K	B
P	T	C	N	E	H	E	P	A	Y	B
H	U	I	R	N	K	O	C	B	U	L
F	E	B	O	A	R	S	B	G	E	P
A	E	R	A	G	S	E	T	O	Q	J
U	T	U	E	I	T	O	T	F	R	L
H	Q	E	M	D	L	S	U	R	E	K
E	R	E	B	R	I	P	E	Z	A	T
G	I	I	E	E	I	V	I	O	Z	P
Y	W	D	F	P	T	W	O	T	S	M
S	E	O	H	T	T	G	D	B	E	E

The sorted sequences are:

8 15 5 4 9 1 7 6 10 3 25 2:
eight, fifteen, five, four, nine, one, seven, six, ten, three, twenty-five, two

Wednesday, Tuesday, Thursday, Saturday, Monday, Friday

January, March, May, February, December, April, August, June

>> Week Seven

> Visualisation

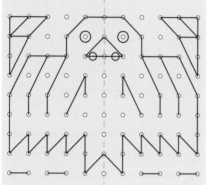

The minimum set of patterns is: 2, 3 and 7.

> Reasoning

3	6	4	5	1	2
4	2	6	1	5	3
5	1	2	3	4	6
2	5	1	6	3	4
6	3	5	4	2	1
1	4	3	2	6	5

4	5	3	6	1	2
2	1	4	5	6	3
6	3	1	2	4	5
5	2	6	1	3	4
1	4	2	3	5	6
3	6	5	4	2	1

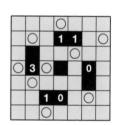

> Numbers

$(5 \times (7-2) \times 3) + 25 = 100$

$((25+7) \times 5) + (3 \times 2) = 166$

You can solve this puzzle using simultaneous equations, or just by guessing if you prefer! Andrew is 5, Bradley is 7 and Charlie is 12.

> Words

TENNIS, BASKETBALL, SWIMMING, BOXING

RASHER DASHED SASHES
BIB DID GIG PIP SIS TIT
SINGES DINGED RINGER
TROT GROG PROP (you might also have CROC)

TEAT DEAD REAR SEAS
HASH EASE SASS
NOUN TOUT

> Visualisation

The pattern pairs are:
1 and 2
3 and 7
4 and 5
6 and 8

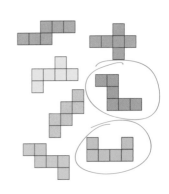

> Reasoning

3	4	5	8	2	7	6	1
7	2	1	6	3	8	5	4
4	3	2	7	6	1	8	5
1	6	8	5	7	4	2	3
2	7	3	1	5	6	4	8
8	5	6	4	1	2	3	7
6	8	7	3	4	5	1	2
5	1	4	2	8	3	7	6

1	4	6	3	5	2	7	8
5	2	7	8	4	3	6	1
3	1	5	7	8	6	4	2
4	6	8	2	1	5	3	7
7	5	3	1	2	4	8	6
2	8	4	6	7	1	5	3
8	3	1	5	6	7	2	4
6	7	2	4	3	8	1	5

6♣	10♠
4♦	3♥

> Memory

The missing fruit is:

> Numbers

⁷⁺ 1	⁸⁺ 5	¹⁰⁺ 6	4	⁵⁺ 3	2
6	2	1	¹⁹⁺ 3	4	5
¹⁻ 2	¹⁻ 4	5	1	6	³ˣ 3
3	⁵⁷⁶ˣ 6	4	³⁻ 2	5	1
4	3	2	¹⁰ˣ 5	1	²⁴ˣ 6
⁵÷ 5	1	²÷ 3	6	2	4

Burst balloons to leave
the following sums:
$28 = 17 + 7 + 4$
$44 = 32 + 12$
$41 = 22 + 12 + 7$
$50 = 22 + 17 + 7 + 4$

> Words

A	P	P	L	E		H	I	C	K	O	R	Y				
P		A					I			O			P	E	A	R
R	O	W	A	N			T			S			C			
I		P		U		H	O	R	N	B	E	A	M			
C		A		T		E		U		W		E		C		
O		W		M	I	M	O	S	A		O		E		L	I
T				E		L			C	O	O	L	A	B	A	H
	M	A	G	N	O	L	I	A		D		L		E		
	A			C			C			E						
A	P	P	L	E		K			I		P	R	U	N	U	S
S	L		L					A				C				
H	E	L	M				A	C	A	C	I	A				

The words are:
INTELLIGENT
ASSIMILATE
TRANSCENDENTAL
OBFUSCATION
CLAUSTROPHOBIC

> Visualisation

The resulting colours are:
Green
Orange
Purple

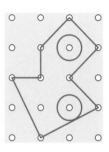

> Reasoning

Option b - in each case the pattern rotates 90 degrees clockwise

> Memory

The changed words are highlighted:
There once was a **gorgeous**, yellow duckling. He was very proud of his **beautiful**, fluffy feathers. Even when it **poured**, the **rain splashed** off his back like **water** off a human's umbrella. His little **ducky** feet **paddled** him from A to **Z**, and he lived happily forever on his **pond**.

> Numbers

The brain chain results are:

27
72
37
72
105

> 4 fence posts
> 10 fence posts
> 6 fence posts

> Words

The following words can be found:
CENT, CITE, CONTENT, CONTINENT, COT, COTE, INNOCENT,
INTENT, INTO, INTONE, NET, NIT, NOT, NOTE, NOTICE, OCTET,
TEN, TENON, TENT, TIE, TIN, TINE, TINT, TIT, TOE, TON, TONE,
TONIC, TONNE, TOT, TOTE

The quotations are:

Only those who dare to fail greatly can ever achieve greatly.
Robert F Kennedy

Beauty is truth, and truth is beauty
John Keats

The greater the obstacle, the more glory in overcoming it.
Moliere

It is never too late to be what you might have been.
George Eliot

> Visualisation

The missing piece is number 4.

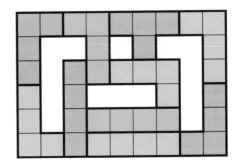

> Reasoning

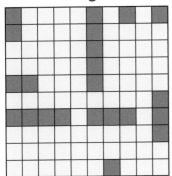

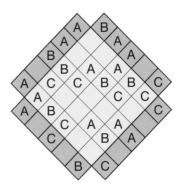

> Memory

The original balloons are those that haven't been recoloured white here.

> 11 balloons in the picture
> Yellow balloons are the most frequent
> There is only one turquoise balloon, one blue balloon, one purple balloon and one orange balloon.

> Numbers

31	27	23	19	21
29	25	21	17	11
33	39	43	13	15
37	41	19	15	19
49	45	21	25	29

31	27	23	19	21
29	25	21	17	11
33	39	43	13	15
37	41	19	15	19
49	45	21	25	29

The longest path for "-2" is 11 squares long.

The secret to a puzzle like this is to work out how to progressively obtain different volumes of liquid, step by step. The shortest solution requires 7 steps:

Pour C into B for 0, 5, 3
Pour B into A for 3, 2, 3
Pour A into C for 0, 2, 6
Pour B into A for 2, 0, 6
Pour C into B for 2, 5, 1
Pour B into A for 3, 4, 1
Pour A into C for 0, 4, 4

> Words

A, ME, TELL, TENOR, DELUDES, AGNOSTIC

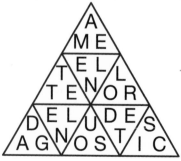

The following words can be made by the word slider:

MANED, MANES, MARES, MARTS, MEMES, MERES, MIMED, MIMES, MINED, MINES, MINTS, MINTY, MIRED, MIRES, NAMED, NAMES, NANNY, NARES, NENES, NINES, NINNY, OARED

> Visualisation

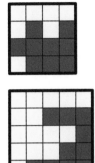

The face counts are:

Blue or brown eyes	12
A red or yellow nose	5
An eye patch	3
Symmetrical eyebrows	9
Smiling or unhappy mouths	11
Red eyes **and** a yellow nose	2

> Reasoning

2	4	3	1	5
5	1	2	3	4
1	3	4	5	2
4	5	1	2	3
3	2	5	4	1

2	3	4	5	1
5	1	3	4	2
4	2	1	3	5
3	5	2	1	4
1	4	5	2	3

> Memory

> The play was written by Sophocles in around 430BC
> The Riddle of the Sphinx
> Arthur Wynne
> Word-Cross
> 1913 in the New York World
> The Sunday Express
> 2004
> The US

> Numbers

The pairs are:

2-4, 3-6, 7-14, 8-16, 9-18 and 12-24

4-11, 5-12, 8-15, 10-17, 18-25, 24-31

6-2, 9-3, 15-5, 36-12, 81-27, 54-18

> Words

Acacia
Amaryllis
Snapdragon
Narcissus
Snowdrop
Petunia
Azalea
Aster
Rose
Edelweiss
Sweet pea
Allium
Mallow

Words that can be found include:
ACCORD, ACCORDION, ACID, ADO, ARC, CAD, CAR, CARD,
COD, CODA, CON, COO, COR, CORD, CORDON, CROON,
DOC, DON, DONOR, DOOR, ICON, ION, NOD, NOR,
RACCOON (or RACOON), RAD, RADON, RADIO, ROC, ROOD

> Visualisation

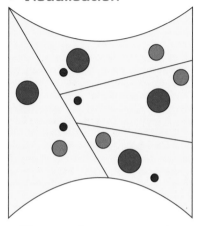

> Reasoning

	1	2	4	4	2	
1	5	4	2	1	3	3
2	4	5	1	3	2	3
5	1	2	3	4	5	1
4	2	3	4	5	1	2
2	3	1	5	2	4	2
	3	3	1	2	2	

	1	2	2	3	2	
1	5	3	4	1	2	3
5	1	2	3	4	5	1
2	4	5	1	2	3	2
3	2	4	5	3	1	3
2	3	1	2	5	4	2
	3	3	2	1	2	

Too big for your boots

There's something between us / Something has come between us

> Memory

The cherries, squash, cucumber and plum disappear; the onion, pea pod, pineapple and pumpkin are new.

> Numbers

4	×	2	×	1	=	8
+		+		×		
5	−	3	×	8	=	16
×		×		×		
9	−	7	×	6	=	12
=		=		=		
81		35		48		

1	5	3	6	2	4
4	2	6	1	3	5
5	1	2	4	6	3
3	6	4	2	5	1
6	4	5	3	1	2
2	3	1	5	4	6

> Words

> He needed to RESHIP the fruit before it began to PERISH.
> In what SECTOR of the shop would she find a CORSET?
> The steady clip-clop of the CART-HORSE sounded to its owner like the finest ORCHESTRA.
> Observing the latest UPTREND, it was PRUDENT to buy.
> He tried to play the ORGAN, but all he heard was a strange GROAN.
> It took some effort to get ORGANISED, but it was the most GRANDIOSE event.
> To finalise the settlement, the SENORITA needed to NOTARISE the documents.

KITTEN: young of the animal
BOWL: a typical place to store the object
WATCH: what you do with the object
LAMP: the most essential component of the item
STEAMER: something that can be propelled by the object

> Visualisation

Pyramid c.

> There are 6 blue shapes
> There are 5 four-sided shapes
> There are 4 triangular shapes

> Reasoning

1	3	4	4	6	5	6
5	1	3	6	3	2	4
1	7	2	4	3	4	7
5	4	5	1	5	7	5
3	7	6	4	7	4	2
7	5	4	2	1	6	3
6	5	1	1	4	3	2

17	18	24	25	27	28	29	30	31
16	19	23	26	73	72	35	34	32
15	20	22	76	75	74	71	36	33
13	14	21	77	79	81	70	68	37
11	12	8	7	78	80	69	67	38
10	9	3	1	6	64	65	66	39
53	55	2	4	5	63	62	61	40
52	54	56	57	58	59	60	44	41
51	50	49	48	47	46	45	43	42

> Numbers

The 3×3 grid makes 9 1×1 squares, 4 2×2 squares and 1 3×3 square for a total of 14 squares.

A 4×4 grid adds 16 more to give a total of 30 squares.

A 5×5 grid would therefore contain an additional 25 for a total of 55 squares.

In general the total number of squares in the grid is the sum of the squares from 1 to the size of the grid 'x by x', that is $1^2 + 2^2 + ... + (x-1)^2 + x^2$. The sum of this series is in fact equal to $(x(x+1)(2x+1))/6$.

24× 6	4	**9+** 2	1	3	**30×** 5
1− 1	5	3	**2÷** 4	2	6
15+ 4	3	**3−** 5	2	**3÷** 6	1
5	6	**3÷** 1	3	**16×** 4	2
5+ 3	**12×** 2	6	**120×** 5	1	4
2	1	4	6	**15×** 5	3

> Words

PARTED, DRAGOON, BARONET, PIRATE, PEARL, DREAD, FROND, TRUST, GYRATE, TROUGHS, THRUST, CLOUD

Possible word chain solutions are:

FACE	CUTE	NICE
FARE	CURE	MICE
DARE	CARE	MIRE
DARN	BARE	MARE
DAWN	BARK	MARS
DOWN	BACK	EARS

> Creativity

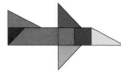

> Visualisation

The top picture has 15 cubes on its top row, 15 on its middle row and 10 on its bottom row for a total of **40 cubes**.

The bottom picture has 11 cubes on the top row, 14 on the 2nd row, 14 on the 3rd row, 13 on the 4th row, 17 on the 5th row and 16 on the bottom row for a total of **85 cubes.**

> Reasoning

> Memory

The differences are:
Red sign has become pink
Sun has appeared in sky
Extra hill has appeared at back left
Field on left now has bushes on all 4 sides
The fence on the right has vanished
The central road markings change colour

> Numbers

				6	3	23		
		16	5	6	2	1	3	
	16 15	6	1	3	2	4	29	
10	3	2	4	1	10	7	3	15
12	8	4	11		23	9	8	6
7	4	1	2		16	17 3	2	1
	4	3	1	26 16	2	9	7	8
		35	5	7	6	8	9	
		20	3	9	8			

> Total calories for the day is 2200
> I'd need to walk 2²/₃ miles
> I should eat 75%
> I'd have eaten 318 calories less

> Words

1) ARMS   ALMS
2) DRAFT   DRAUGHT
3) CURB   KERB
4) CYMBAL   SYMBOL
5) MAYOR   MARE
6) PACKED   PACT
7) MIGHT   MITE
8) SHOOT   CHUTE

TENNIS
SQUASH

POTATO
CARROT

CAMERA
TRIPOD

SHINING
RADIANT

> Visualisation

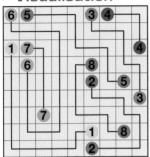

> A cube has 12 edges and 8 corners
> You can see no more than 9 edges
(unless you use a mirror!)
> 5 faces on a square-based pyramid
> 6 faces - it would be a cuboid
> 10 faces on the resulting shape
(2 for the top plus bottom,
and 8 around the sides)

> Reasoning

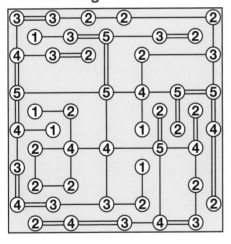

4	2	5	3	6	1
6	5	2	1	3	4
2	1	3	4	5	6
5	3	1	6	4	2
3	6	4	2	1	5
1	4	6	5	2	3

2	5	3	1	6	4
6	1	4	2	3	5
1	4	5	6	2	3
3	2	6	4	5	1
4	3	2	5	1	6
5	6	1	3	4	2

> Memory

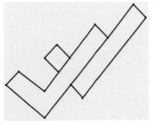

Two ticks (check marks)

> Numbers

256: multiply the previous two numbers together
23: add 1, add 2, add 3, etc (add one more each time)
90: subtract 8, subtract 7, subtract 6, etc (subtract one less each time)
64: add 3, add 5, add 7 etc (add two more each time)
9: divide the previous number by 2
50: each number is x^2+1, for values of x=1, 2, 3, 4, 5, etc.
   Alternatively the sequence is add 3, add 5, add 7, add 9, etc.

$$65 = 29 + 10 + 26$$
$$75 = 10 + 30 + 35$$
$$85 = 29 + 30 + 26$$

> Words

CHAIR
TABLE
SOFA
BED
SHELF
WARDROBE

The pairs are:

RELISH	ENJOY
SAUCE	CHEEK
CONSTANT	ENDURING
FIXED	CORRECTED
MARKED	NOTED

WONDER	GENIUS
THINK	REFLECT
MIRROR	EMULATE
FOLLOW	SUCCEED
PROSPER	FLOURISH

> Visualisation

The hidden characters are a 5 and a 1, making '51'.

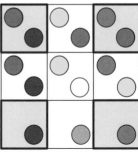

Each white square is formed by overlapping all neighbouring pairs of adjacent squares. If two circles overlap then the result is the colour of light that would be formed if two lights of the original colours were merged.

> Reasoning

You can solve this via logic, or experimentation works too. Logically you can see that Pete and Simon can't both be telling the truth since they contradict one another. Therefore Dan must be telling the truth: it was Simon.

> Memory

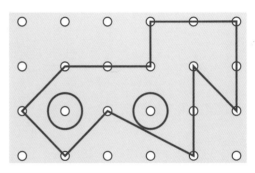

>> Week Sixteen

> Numbers

²⁻ -1	-3	⁶⁻ -2	3	⁰⁺ 1	¹⁻ 2
³⁺ 1	2	¹÷ -3	-1	-2	3
³⁻ -2	1	3	¹²ˣ -3	2	-1
³⁻ 3	-2	-1	2	⁴⁻ -3	1
⁵⁻ 2	3	²÷ 1	-2	³ˣ -1	-3
-3	-1	2	1	¹⁺ 3	-2

$(((4 \times 7) + 9) \times 2) + 75 = \mathbf{149}$

$((2 + 9) \times 75) + (4 \times 7) = \mathbf{853}$

> Words

PETS	STEP
MINED	DENIM
REWARD	DRAWER
DELIVER	REVILED
STRESSED	DESSERTS

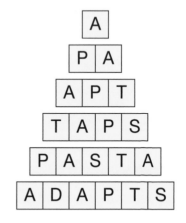

> Visualisation

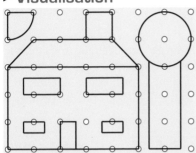

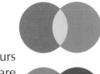

The colours formed are yellow, cyan and magenta.

> Reasoning

3	2	4	6	1	5
6	4	1	5	2	3
5	1	3	2	6	4
2	6	5	3	4	1
4	5	6	1	3	2
1	3	2	4	5	6

5	4	6	2	1	3
1	2	5	3	6	4
3	6	4	1	2	5
6	5	2	4	3	1
2	3	1	5	4	6
4	1	3	6	5	2

The phrases are:

Never in a month of Sundays

The end of the line

> Memory

The differences are: the ground changes from brown to black; the yellow part of the sunset becomes orange; the bottom-left of the tree grows extra branches; some birds nests appear at the top-right of the tree; a small hillock appears on the ground to the right.

> Numbers

The square is the lightest object. The star is the heaviest object.

The results are 46, 58, 105, 115 and 180.

> Words

ASSESSES; OUTVOTE; KNEEL; MAXIMUM; AGGRAVATE

AIRLINE; BRACELET; BUTTERFLY; CATWALK; COWBOY; DOWNTURN; FORTUNE; TREADMILL; UPSET

> Visualisation

The pairs are 1&5, 2&6, 3&7 and 4&8.

You can't draw it with a single stroke. For example consider the small diamond/rotated square in the bottom centre - you would need to visit this twice to draw both it and the lines holding it either side, but this can't be done due to the triangle it is in the centre of.

> Reasoning

2	5	4	1	3	6	7
6	1	7	5	4	3	2
4	3	6	2	7	1	5
1	2	3	7	5	4	6
3	7	5	6	1	2	4
5	4	2	3	6	7	1
7	6	1	4	2	5	3

1	6	2	4	7	5	3
7	4	6	5	2	3	1
2	3	5	1	6	4	7
5	2	1	3	4	7	6
6	5	7	2	3	1	4
3	1	4	7	5	6	2
4	7	3	6	1	2	5

The next in the sequence is 'c'. At each stage the star gets darker and gains an extra point. The yellow snail shell rotates clockwise around the outer edge.

> Memory

The orderings are 4 6 5 1 2 3; 5 2 3 7 6 4 1; 7 8 4 6 2 1 5 3.

> Numbers

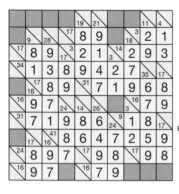

> 1 in 6, because it doesn't matter what you roll first but you then have a 1 in 6 chance of rolling it again.

> Again, the first roll doesn't matter but then you have a 1 in 6 chance each time. You therefore have a 1 in 6 times 1 in 6 chance = 1 in 36.

> There are 36 possible results from rolling 2 dice: 6x6 = 36. Of these, 6 give a total of "7": 1+6, 2+5, 3+4, 4+3, 5+2 and 6+1. So the chance is 6 in 36 = 1 in 6.

> It doesn't matter that in the past you have rolled four dice and had a particular result. Starting from now your likelihood of rolling the same number again next is still 1 in 6. So the answer is 1 in 6.

> Words

Words that can be found include:
ACE, ACRE, ACT, APT, ARC, ARE, CAP, CAPTURE, CAR, CARE, CARER, CAT, CREATURE, CUR, CURE, CURER, CURT, CUT, EAR, EAT, ECRU, ERA, ERE, ERECT, ERR, PACE, PACER, PACT, PAR, PARE, PAT, RACE, RACER, RAP, RAPT, RAPTURE, RAT, REACT, REAP, RECAP, RECAPTURE, RECUR, RUT, TAP, TAR, TARE, TRUCE

> Visualisation

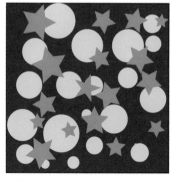

> There are 20 yellow circles.
> There are 17 orange stars.
> There are 5 circles which aren't overlapped by a star.

> Reasoning

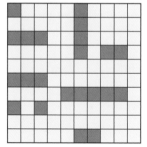

5	6	0	6	2	5	1	1
2	4	3	5	1	1	6	6
2	3	6	1	6	0	2	1
0	0	0	0	2	4	2	0
5	1	3	4	4	3	5	4
4	4	2	5	3	2	6	3
0	5	5	1	4	3	3	6

> Memory

The missing vegetables are:

> Numbers

This puzzle can be solved using simultaneous equations, or simply by experimentation if you prefer. Andrea is 3, Barbara is 5, Christina is 8 and Debbie is 11.

> The total length of all twelve edges is (12m×4) + (3m×4) + (4m×4) = 76m.

> The volume of space is 12m × 3m × 4m = 144m³

> The longest rod would fit in the longest diagonal, so the question is how long is this diagonal, from the near-top-left to the far-bottom-right corner? A diagonal across the floor only would be 5m long, since the diagonal across the 3m by 4m floor forms the long side of a right-angled triangle and Pythagoras tells us that the square of the length of the longest side of a right-angled triangle (the hypotenuse) is equal to the sum of the squares of the shorter sides: $3^2+4^2 = 5^2$. Next we have another right-angled triangle formed by the diagonal across the floor and the height of the unit, so with sides 5m and 12m the longest diagonal (the hypotenuse) is 13m, since $5^2+12^2 = 13^2$. So the longest straight rod that can possibly fit would be 13m long.

> Words

The following words can all be found:
ALE, AND, ANT, ARE, ART, ATE, ELD, END, ERE, IRE, OLD, OLE, ONE, ORE, UTE

> The STUDENT didn't do much work, so his learning was STUNTED.

> She studied the SCHEMATIC that outlined the details of her CATECHISM.

> The first EARTH-BORN aliens looked oddly ABHORRENT.

> Instead of being CREATIVE, the agency ended up being REACTIVE.

> There was a TANGIBLE noise; the sound of BLEATING.

> He hid in AMONG the MANGO trees.

> She found the STEADIEST boat to take her STATESIDE.

> Visualisation

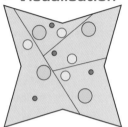

The missing piece is number 2

> Reasoning

1		3		3		2	
3		1		1		1	1
3	2				2	2	
2		2	2		3		
		2		2	2		3
	1	0				1	1
3	1		0		3		2
3		3		1		1	

5	3	7	4	8	2	1	5
1	6	6	8	3	4	2	7
6	4	8	7	1	3	5	3
2	6	6	1	6	5	6	4
6	5	2	4	7	3	8	3
7	6	5	2	4	1	4	8
4	1	8	5	2	3	7	6
5	6	4	3	1	7	1	1

> Numbers

$^{1÷}$2	$^{21×}$7	3	$^{5×}$5	1	$^{21+}$6	4
3	6	$^{33+}$7	$^{1-}$1	2	4	5
$^{90×}$6	5	1	$^{28×}$7	4	2	$^{6×}$3
$^{2-}$7	3	4	6	5	$^{7×}$1	2
5	$^{12+}$4	$^{3÷}$6	2	3	7	1
1	2	$^{9+}$5	4	7	$^{126×}$3	6
4	1	$^{6×}$2	3	$^{30×}$6	5	7

```
                  130
             59        71
          28     31        40
       15     13     18     22
     8     7     6     12     10
   2     6     1     5     7     3
```

> Words

ADMIRE, RAMMED, RAMMER, RAMOSE, RARITY, RATITE, REMISE,
REMOTE, RESITE, RETIED, RETIRE, RUMMER, SAMITE, SARNEY,
SATIRE, SETOSE, SUMMED, SUMMER, TERMED, TURNED, TURNER

The missing pairs are: MM, LO, TR, OO, EW and MP.

> Visualisation

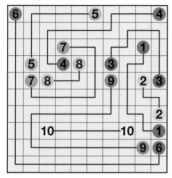

The overlaid words are:
problem reading
colour overlay
genuine glasses
three words here

> Reasoning

	1	3	2	2	4	2	
1	6	2	5	3	1	4	3
3	4	5	6	1	2	3	2
2	5	1	3	6	4	2	3
5	2	3	4	5	6	1	2
4	3	4	1	2	5	6	1
2	1	6	2	4	3	5	2
	4	1	3	3	3	2	

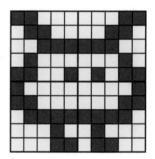

> Memory

R	R	L	D	E	H	R	K	A	R	A	T	E
I	G	G	L	R	S	A	O	P	V	D	G	C
S	H	N	N	A	E	S	N	W	O	N	V	I
A	N	I	I	I	B	S	O	D	I	L	I	S
A	T	L	C	C	V	Y	S	R	B	N	O	G
G	E	G	R	O	N	I	E	A	C	A	G	N
N	U	N	I	G	R	E	D	L	G	A	L	I
I	Q	A	C	V	T	M	F	Y	L	E	L	L
I	O	T	K	N	I	E	T	L	K	O	W	W
K	R	T	E	N	N	I	S	T	O	S	V	O
S	C	I	T	S	A	N	M	Y	G	G	D	B
O	R	O	Y	R	E	H	C	R	A	U	R	O
O	N	O	H	T	A	R	A	M	J	C	A	O

> Numbers

$((4+7) \times 50) + (6 \div 3) = 552$
$(50 + 4) \times (6 + 7) \div 3 = 234$

> The first generation has 6 children. Each of these have 5 children for 30 children in the next generation. Then each of these has 4 children for a final total of 120 children, each of which has one zog. So the answer is 120 zogs.
> From the oldest to the youngest generation there are 2 + 12 + 60 + 120 people in Zox's family for a total of 194 people.
> If there had been twice as many children then in each generation in turn there would have been 12, 120 and 960 children per generation respectively, so in other words there'd be 960 zogs now.

> Words

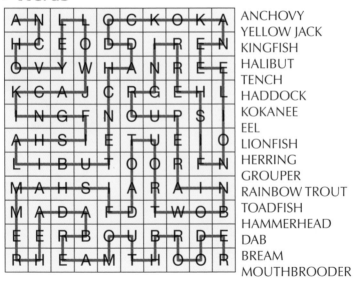

ANCHOVY
YELLOW JACK
KINGFISH
HALIBUT
TENCH
HADDOCK
KOKANEE
EEL
LIONFISH
HERRING
GROUPER
RAINBOW TROUT
TOADFISH
HAMMERHEAD
DAB
BREAM
MOUTHBROODER

Pluto - the only one not classified as a "planet" (it is a dwarf planet);
Pluto - the only one who is not a Greek god (he is a Roman god);
Magnolia - the only one usually classified as a tree, not a shrub;
Entangle - all of the other words are anagrams of one another.

> Visualisation

The minimum set is 4, 5, 6 and 8.

A1, B2, C3

> Reasoning

4	7	3	1	6	2	5	8	9
1	8	5	9	4	3	7	6	2
9	6	2	5	8	7	3	1	4
2	9	8	4	7	5	6	3	1
5	1	6	3	2	8	4	9	7
7	3	4	6	9	1	2	5	8
8	4	1	7	5	6	9	2	3
3	5	9	2	1	4	8	7	6
6	2	7	8	3	9	1	4	5

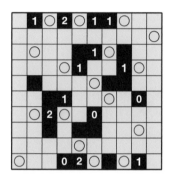

> Memory

The differences are: Sun beams lose the yellow glow; flowers change from red to yellow; blue vehicle appears on the left; the top-left cloud vanishes; the small plants disappear at the bottom left; the far-right centre hillock changes colour to leaf green.

> Numbers

$$89 = 49 + 19 + 21$$
$$99 = 28 + 28 + 43$$
$$109 = 49 + 28 + 32$$

> Words

Words that can be found include:
COIN, CON, CUR, CURIO, ICON, INCUR, ION, IONIC, RUIN, RUM, RUN, RUNIC, URIC, ZINC, ZIRCONIUM

1) MESS + AGES = MESSAGES
2) CONS + TABLE = CONSTABLE
3) MISER + ABLE = MISERABLE
4) PER + SON = PERSON
5) CUP + BOARD = CUPBOARD

> Creativity

The pictures shown can be formed like this:

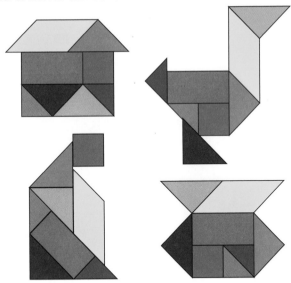

> Visualisation

You really can draw 18 different squares and an additional 45 non-square rectangles!

> Reasoning

5	3	4	6	2	1
1	5	2	3	4	6
6	1	3	4	5	2
2	6	5	1	3	4
4	2	1	5	6	3
3	4	6	2	1	5

6	1	3	2	4	5
1	3	6	5	2	4
4	2	1	3	5	6
3	5	4	6	1	2
5	6	2	4	3	1
2	4	5	1	6	3

The first phrase is the trickiest:
Great minds think alike

The second is:
Hanging on every word

> Numbers

The brain chain results are:
504
183
245
188
168

¹⁴4	²³9	¹⁰3	7	²⁴6	⁷5	2	⁹8	1
2	8	⁴1	3	4	9	5	¹³7	6
5	6	¹⁵7	8	³2	1	¹⁶9	3	4
3	¹³2	6	5	²⁹8	7	⁵4	1	²³9
²¹9	5	⁶4	2	1	¹⁰3	7	⁶6	8
7	⁹1	8	4	9	¹⁴6	3	5	¹⁷2
¹⁵6	4	5	⁴1	3	¹⁰2	8	¹⁵9	7
¹¹8	3	²⁷9	6	7	⁵4	1	2	5
⁸1	7	¹¹2	9	5	¹⁴8	6	4	3

> Words

H	I	S	T	O	R	Y		I	S		T	H	E
	V	E	R	S	I	O	N		O	F		P	A
S	T		E	V	E	N	T	S		T	H	A	T
	P	E	O	P	L	E		H	A	V	E		D
E	C	I	D	E	D		T	O		A	G	R	E
E		U	P	O	N		N	A	P	O	L	E	O
N		B	O	N	A	P	A	R	T	E			

History is the version of past events that people have decided to agree upon. *Napoleon Bonaparte*

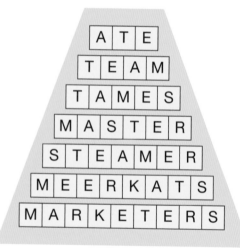